Mel Bay Presents

☆ SONGS OF THE ☆ AMERICAN PEOPLE

By Jerry Silverman

Cover illustration by Greg Ragland.

INTERN.   TED IN U.S.A.

Contents

New England

New England

Old Lyme, Connecticut. Courtesy of N.Y. Public Library Picture Collection.

The Battle of Stonington

On August 9, 1814, a British naval squadron under Commodore Sir Thomas Masterman Hardy appeared off Stonington and instructed the town authorities to have the place vacated, as it would be destroyed in an hour. The town selectmen replied that they would defend Stonington to the end. The ensuing British bombardment was answered so effectively by the local militia that after three futile days the British were forced to withdraw.

By Philip Freneau

Three gal–lant ships from Eng–land came,
Freight–ed deep with fire and flame, And oth–er things we
need not name, To have a dash at Ston–ing–ton. Now
safe ar–rived, they work be–gun; They tho't to make the Yan–kees run, And

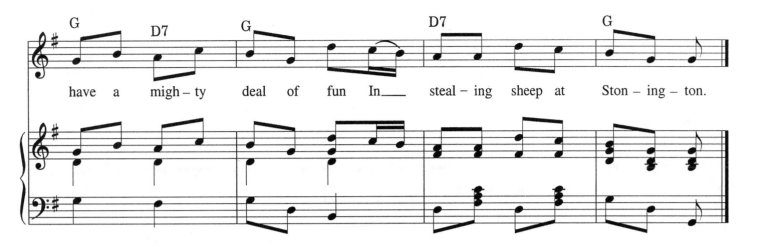

have a migh–ty deal of fun In___ steal – ing sheep at Ston – ing – ton.

A Yankee then popped up his head,
And Parson Jones our sarmon read,
In which our Reverend Doctor said
That they must fight for Stonington.
Their ships advancing several ways,
The Britons soon began to blaze,
Which put old Williams in amaze,
Who feared the loss of Stonington.

The *Ramilies* first began the attack,
And *Nimrod* made a mighty crack,
And none can tell what kept them back
From setting fire to Stonington.
Their bombs were thrown, their rockets flew,
And not a man of all their crew,
Though every man stood full in view,
Could kill a man of Stonington.

Their old razee, with red-hot ball,
Soon made a farmer's barrack fall,
And did a cow-house sadly maul,
That stood a mile from Stonington.
We Yankees to our fort repaired,
And made as how we little cared
About their shot, though very hard
They blazed away at Stonington.

They killed a goose, they killed a hen,
Three hogs they wounded in a pen;
They dashed away - and pray, what then?
That was not taking Stonington.
The shells were thrown, the rockets flew,
But not a shell of all they threw,
Though every house was in full view,
Could burn a house in Stonington.

To have a turn we thought but fair.
We Yankees brought two guns to bear,
And, sir, it would have made you stare
To have seen the smoke at Stonington.
We bored the *Nimrod* through and through,
And killed and mangled half her crew,
When, riddled, crippled, she withdrew
And cursed the boys of Stonington.

The *Ramilies* then gave up the fray,
And with her comrades sneaked away;
Such was the valor on that day
Of British tars at Stonington.
Now, some assart on sartin grounds,
Beside their damage and their wounds,
It cost the king ten thousand pounds
To have a fling at Stonington.

The Leatherman

Between 1860 and 1889 the Old Leatherman was a familiar sight in eastern Connecticut and western New York. Winter and summer, always dressed in clothing made out of scraps of leather, he trudged along the Connecticut River, through the shore towns, up the Hudson to Poughkeepsie, and across through Thomaston and Farmington to the Connecticut River again — never varying his direction or itinerary — completing his circuit once every 41 days. No one knew what compelled him to wander thus, accepting food from local inhabitants but never speaking to anyone. He spent his nights in caves or shelters. He perished in one of his caves during a snowstorm in March 1889. His grave is in Rye, New York. In this song, his route is extended all the way to Maine, although he never went that far.

Connecticut

Leath-er – man, Leath-er – man, why do you go?
{ The winds they do whis–tle, the
{ The way is all froz – en and

winds they do blow. Yes, the winds they do whis–tle and blow. snow. I've
lad – en with snow. Yes, the way is all lad–en with

trav–elled the o – cean, I've trav–elled the sea. And I'm trav–el – ing back my dear

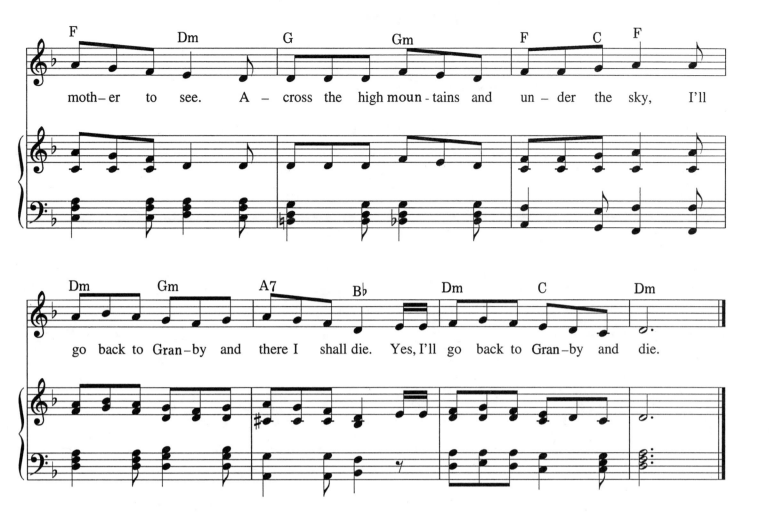

mother to see. A – cross the high mountains and under the sky, I'll go back to Granby and there I shall die. Yes, I'll go back to Granby and die.

Then, Leatherman, Leatherman, tell me your name,
And why you do go through the forest and plain,
Through the lonesome forest and plain.
Then, Leatherman, Leatherman, tell me your name,
And why you do travel from Essex to Maine,
On the road between Essex and Maine.
The sky is my roof and the grass is my bed,
I'll live till I die and I'll die till I'm dead.
I cannot remember the sound of my name
Or why I am clad in the animal skein,
All clad in the animal skein.

Then, Leatherman, Leatherman, tarry awhile,
From your mumbling, stumbling wearisome mile,
From your stumbling wearisome mile.
Then Leatherman, Leatherman, tarry awhile,
And tell me the reason you never do smile
And why then you never do smile.
My body is aching and wracked with pain,
My soul is in torment and burning with shame,
The cause of my torture I never can tell,
As I tread this cruel road between heaven and hell,
On the road between heaven and hell.

Moosehead Lake

Variants of this rough-and-tumble lumberjack song are found wherever the tigers of the woods set up camp. In the Adirondack Mountains of New York, a similar ballad is entitled "Blue Mountain Lake." The foreman is always the villain, and the cook, the object of scorn and contempt.

Maine

In eight – een hun – dred and nine – ty two, Bant Breau and George El – li – ot they start – ed a crew. They were jol – ly good fel – lows, and make no mis – take, And they land – ed us safe – ly up – on Moose – head

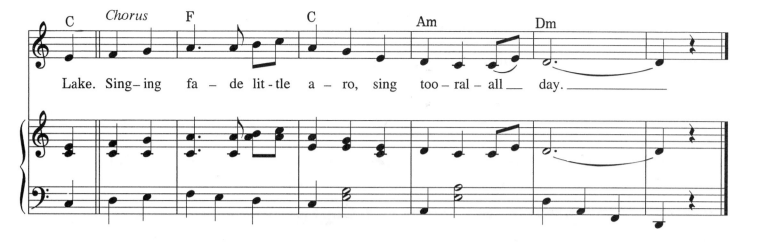

Lake. Sing—ing fa — de lit-tle a — ro, sing too — ral — all __ day. _____

The very next morning we met with the chief,
We soon learned the meaning of sorrow and grief.
We built him a storehouse and likewise a camp,
Lost one of our bold woodsmen all on that wild tramp.   *Chorus*

About five in the morning the cook would sing out,
"Come bullies, come bullies, come bullies turn out."
And some would not mind him, but back they would lay,
And it's "Jesus H. Christ, will you lay there all day?"   *Chorus*

Bill Mitchell, you know, kept our shanty,
And as mean a damn man as you ever did see.
He'd lay around the shanty from morning till night,
And if a man said a word he was ready to fight.   *Chorus*

One morning 'fore daylight, Jim Lou he got mad,
Whipped hell out of Mitchell, and the boys was all glad,
And Bill's wife she stood there, the truth I will tell,
She was tickled to death to see Mitchell catch hell.   *Chorus*

Old Griffin he stood there, the grizzly old drake,
A hand in the racket we feared he would take.
Some of the boys, they pulled him away,
He says, "Fight and be damned, I've nothing to say."   *Chorus*

And then on a Sunday, the boss he would say,
"Your axes go grind, for there's no time to play.
For next Monday morning to the woods you must go,
And forty-five spruce every day you must throw."   *Chorus*

About six in the evenings to the camps we'd all steer,
"Side board the grindstone" was all you could hear.
"Side board the grindstone" for the turns they'd all fight,
And keep the damned old grindstone a-furling all night.   *Chorus*

The Boothbay Whale

When they weren't telling tall tales in the lumber camps, they were telling them along the coast.

Maine

It was way up north in Booth-bay har-bor where the wa-ter's al – ways cold. The

fish – er folk are a clev – er lot, Or so I have been told. Blow

Chorus

hi for his big black head, Blow low for his big black tail. Now

step right up and take a lit – tle swig, And you'll soon see a Booth–bay whale.

They catch their pollack, cod and shad,
By the mouth, the fin or the tail.
One day they got a heck of a jolt,
When into the Bay swam a whale.   *Chorus*

Says Captain Pete, "I've harpooned tuna,
And caught them with my rig,
But I ain't gettin' near no eighty-foot whale,
That fish is too darned big."   *Chorus*

Well, Skipper Jake was a ready man,
Though he had a wooden leg.
Says he, "I think I'll catch that whale,
Let me have that old rum keg."   *Chorus*

Well, he stood on the bow of the *Nancy U,*
And followed that whale for a ride,
And when that whale he surfaced and blowed,
He steered her to starboard side.   *Chorus*

The whale blowed steam from his big spout hole,
While Jake took a slug from his keg;
And before he could dive, Jake jumped on his back,
Hangin' on with his one good leg.   *Chorus*

Well, Jake took his keg and used it like a plug,
Pushed it tight in the old whale's spout,
He kicked it hard, then jumped on board,
Sayin', "Boys, it will never come out."   *Chorus*

Well, the whale he blew, he puffed, he heaved,
And the boys all gave a shout;
And the very next time he 'rose to blow,
He blew his brains right out.   *Chorus*

You bold seafarin' whalermen,
You've wasted all these years,
With race boats, harpoons, ropes and hooks
And all that other gear.   *Chorus*

All you need is a big ol' plug;
Next time you see him spout,
Just kick it in, sit back and rest,
While he blows his brains right out.   *Chorus*

If you ever meet a fisherman from Boothbay, Maine,
And you want to hear a dreadful tale,
Well, step right up and offer him a keg,
And learn how to catch a Boothbay whale.   *Chorus*

Boothbay Harbor, Maine. Courtesy of N.Y. Public Library Picture Collection.

Boston Tea Tax Song

December 16, 1773, was the date of the Boston Tea Party. A group of outraged Bostonians, disguised as "Mohawk Indians," dumped a boatload of tea from British ships into Boston Harbor in response to a threepence-per-pound tax on all tea imported into the Colonies. This unprecedented act of defiance was a link in the chain of events that led inexorably to the Revolutionary War. Contemporary song writers had a field day with the Tea Party.

Squash into the deep descended
Cursed weed of China's coast.
Thus at once our fears were ended—
British rights shall ne'er be lost.

Massachusetts

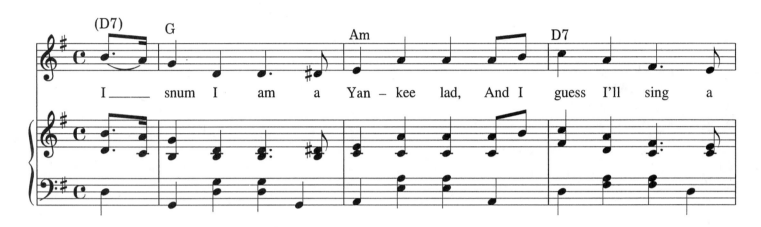

I___ snum I am a Yan – kee lad, And I guess I'll sing a

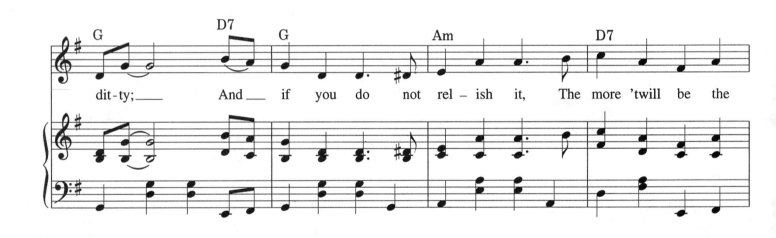

dit-ty;___ And___ if you do not rel – ish it, The more 'twill be the

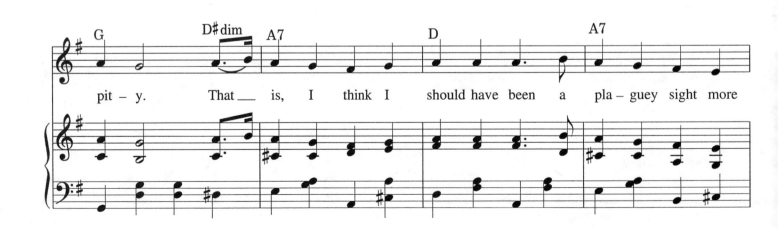

pit – y. That___ is, I think I should have been a pla – guey sight more

14

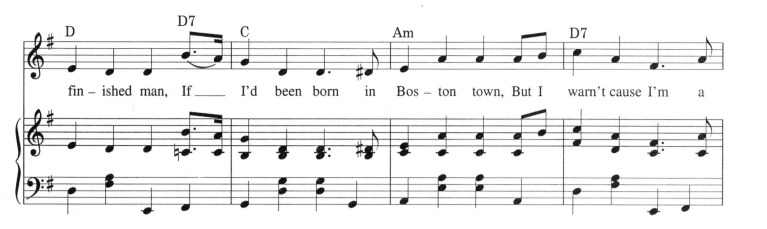

fin – ished man, If ____ I'd been born in Bos – ton town, But I warn't cause I'm a

Chorus

coun-try–man. Tol-le – lol – de rid-dle, Tol-de – lol – de – ray, But I warn't 'cause I'm a coun-try – man.

And t'other day the Yankee folks
Were mad about the taxes,
And so we went like Injuns dressed
To split tea chests with axes.
It was in the year of Seventy-three,
And we felt really gritty.
The Mayor he would have led the gang,
But Boston warn't a city!   *Chorus*

You see we Yankees didn't care
A pin for wealth or booty,
And so in State Street we agreed
We'd never pay the duty;
That is, in State Street 'twould have been,
But 'twas King Street they call'd it then,
And tax on tea, it was so bad,
The women wouldn't scald it then.   *Chorus*

To Charleston Bridge we all went down
To see the thing corrected;
That is, we would have gone there,
But the bridge it warn't erected.
The tea perhaps was very good.
Bohea, Souchong, or Hyson,
But drinking tea it warn't the rage,
The duty made it poison.   *Chorus*

And then aboard the ships we went
Our vengeance to administer,
And we didn't care one tarnal bit
For any king or minister.
We made a plaguey mess of tea
In one of the biggest dishes;
I mean we steeped it in the sea
And treated all the fishes.   *Chorus*

And then you see we were all found out,
A thing we hadn't dreaded.
The leaders were to London sent
And instantly beheaded;
That is, I mean they would have been
If ever they'd been taken.
But the leaders they were never cotch'd,
And so they saved their bacon.   *Chorus*

Now heaven bless the president
And all this goodly nation.
And doubly bless our Boston Mayor
And all the corporation;
And may all those who are our foes,
Or at our praise have falter'd,
Soon have a change - that is, I mean
May all of them get halter'd.   *Chorus*

Bread and Roses

New Year's Day, 1912, ushered in one of the most historic struggles in the history of the American working class. On that cold January 1st, the textile workers of Lawrence, Massachusetts, began a nine-week strike which shook the very foundations of the Bay State and had national repercussions. In its last session, the Massachusetts State Legislature, after tremendous pressure from the workers, had finally passed a law limiting the working hours of children under the age of 18 to 54 hours a week. Needless to say, the huge textile corporations had viciously opposed the law. As an act of retaliation, the employers cut the working hours of all employees to 54 hours a week, with a commensurate cut in wages, of course. The workers in the Lawrence factories, some 35,000 of them, answered this with a complete walk-out.... During a parade through Lawrence, a group of women workers carried banners proclaiming "Bread and Roses!" This poetic presentation of the demands of women workers for equal pay for equal work, together with special consideration as women, echoed throughout the country. (Sing Out, Vol. 2, No. 7, 1957)

Massachusetts

Music by Martha Coleman
Words by James Oppenhem

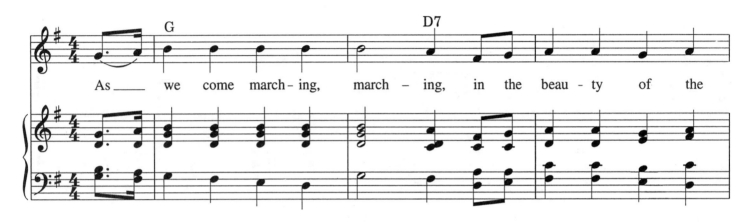

As ___ we come march-ing, march-ing, in the beau-ty of the

day, A ___ mil – lion dark – ened kit – chens, a ___

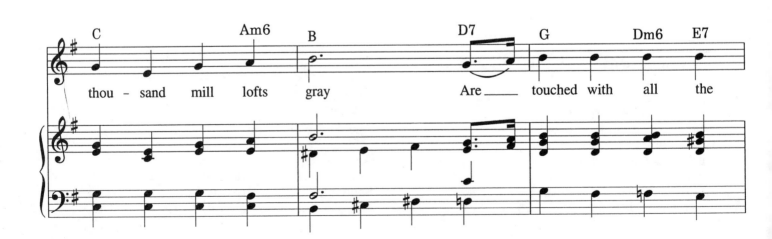

thou – sand mill lofts gray Are ___ touched with all the

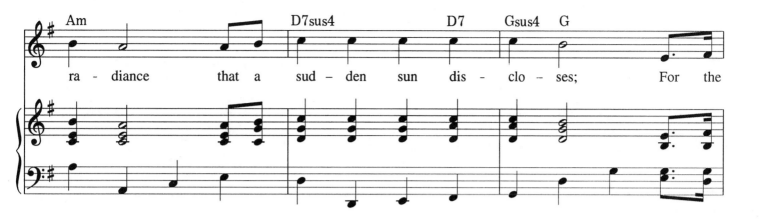

ra - diance that a sud — den sun dis - clo - ses; For the

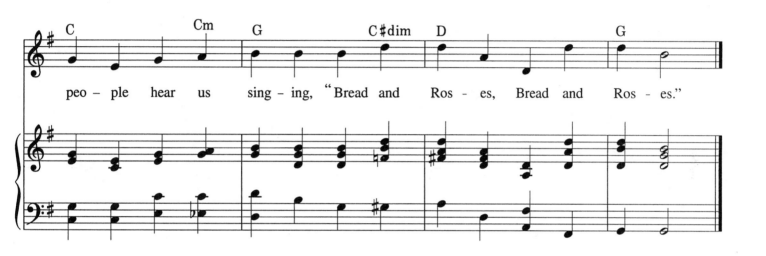

peo — ple hear us sing – ing, "Bread and Ros - es, Bread and Ros - es."

As we come marching, marching, we battle too, for men,
For they are women's children and we mother them again.
Our lives shall not be sweated from birth until life closes.
Hearts starve as well as bodies:
Give us bread, but give us roses.

As we come marching, marching, unnumbered women dead
Go crying through our singing their ancient song of bread.
Small art and love and beauty their drudging spirits knew.
Yes, it is bread that we fight for,
But we fight for roses, too.

As we come marching, marching, we bring the Greater Days,
The rising of the women means the rising of the race.
No more the drudge and idler, ten that toil where one reposes,
But a sharing of life's glories,
Bread and Roses, Bread and Roses.

The Old Granite State

The Singing Hutchinson Family wrote and performed their Abolitionist songs in the 1840s, 1850s, and into the Civil War. This was their "theme song," and they opened every concert with it. In 1844, they were invited to sing for President John Tyler in the White House. They had intended to sing an anti-slavery verse as part of the song, but their congressman, John P. Hale, who had arranged their appearance, begged them not to include the offending verse. They complied, but as the Abolitionist struggle grew sharper, they added more and more anti-slavery songs to their concert programs. The reference to "Emancipation" and "Proclamation" in verse 4 was obviously added to the song much later.

New Hampshire

By Jesse Hutchinson

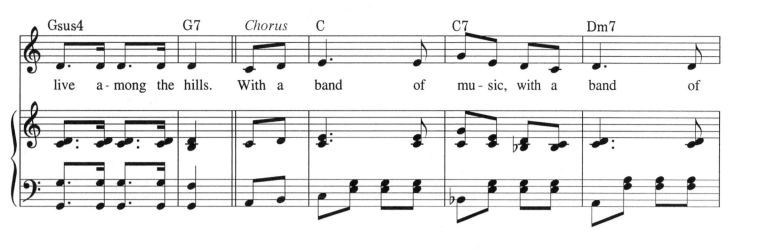

live a-mong the hills. With a band of mu-sic, with a band of

mu-sic, with a band of mu-sic we are pas-sing round the world.

We are all real Yankees,
We are all real Yankees,
We are all real Yankees,
From the Old Granite State.
And by prudent guessing,
And by prudent guessing,
And by prudent guessing,
We shall whittle through the world.   *Chorus*

Liberty is our motto,
Liberty is our motto,
Equal liberty is our motto
In the Old Granite State.
We despise oppression,
We despise oppression,
We despise oppression,
 And we cannot be enslaved. *Chorus*

Yes we're friends of Emancipation
And we'll sing the Proclamation
Till it echoes through our nation
From the Old Granite State.
That the tribe of Jesse,
That the tribe of Jesse,
That the tribe of Jesse,
Are the friends of equal right.   *Chorus*

We are all Washingtonians,
Yes, we're all Washingtonians,
Heav'n bless the Washingtonians,
Of the Old Granite State.
We are all teetotalers,
We are all teetotalers,
We are all teetotalers,
And have signed the Temp'rance Pledge.   *Chorus*

Now three cheers altogether,
Shout Columbia's people ever,
Yankee hearts none can sever,
In the Old Sister States.
Like our Sires before us,
We will swell the chorus,
Till the Heavens o'er us
Shall resound the loud hussa.
Hurrah! Hurrah! Hurrah!   *Chorus*

The Roving Pedlar

This song dates back to at least 1851, when its text appeared in a broadside — a song sheet usually published without music.

New Hampshire

I am a rov–ing ped–lar man, I've roved the coun–try 'round;____ And when I was____ re–solv-ed____ to view some oth–er ground,____ With my pack up-on____ my shoul-der and my cud-gel in my hand,____ I went in-to New Hamp-shire, to view that hand-some land.____

When I came to New Hampshire, the girls all laughed for joy,
The one says to the other, "There's that handsome pedlar boy!"
They invited me to dine with them, they took me by the hand,
And the toasts, they did fly merrily, "Success to the pedlar man!"

I went to Hillsboro County, and there among the maids,
With my old conversation they seemed not dismayed,
While I such fine things sold them, gave them to understand
The humor and good nature of this roving pedlar man.

It's in that Hillsboro County where the girls all dress so neat,
They are kind in every feature and their kisses are so sweet,
There's handsome Jane and Sally, and fair young Betsy too,
Along with one of these fair maids I'll rove the country through.

I went into a tavern, and there all night I stayed,
The landlady's fair daughter of me was not afraid,
She hugged me and she kissed me too, she held me by the hand,
And shyly told her mamma that she loved this pedlar man.

"O daughter, dearest daughter, what do you mean to do?
To rove about the country with a man that you don't know?"
"O mamma, I don't care for that, so do the best you can,
For I'll roam the country over with this roving pedlar man."

It was early in the morning when I was going away,
The landlady's fair daughter to me these words did say,
"How can you be so cru-el, or prove to me unkind,
To go once more a-roving and to leave me here behind?"

Now I'll leave off my peddling and I'll take to me a wife,
For along with this pretty girl I'll surely spend my life.
I'll embrace her late and early, and do the best I can
To cause her for to bless the day she wed the pedlar man.

Portsmouth, New Hampshire, about 1875. Courtesy of N.Y. Public Library Picture Collection.

The Bombardment of Bristol

On October 7, 1775, a small British fleet commanded by Captain James Wallace appeared off Bristol. He was on a foraging mission for the main British fleet anchored in Newport harbor. After a bombardment which lasted an hour and a half, Captain Wallace presented his demands: 200 sheep and 30 cattle. After some negotiation, the matter was settled with the delivery of only 40 sheep.

Rhode Island

In sev- en -teen hun - dred sev-en - ty five, Our Bris - tol town was

much sur - prised, By a thiev – ish

pack of vil - lains who will not work to earn their liv - ings.

October, 'twas the seventh day,
As I have heard the people say,
Wallace - his name be ever cursed,
Come on our harbor just at dusk.

And there his ship did safely moor,
And quickly sent his barge ashore,
With orders that should not be broke,
Or that we might expect a smoke.

Demanding that our magistrates
Should quickly come on board his ship,
And let him have some sheep and cattle,
Or that they might expect a battle.

At eight o'clock by signal given,
Our peaceful atmosphere was riven;
Women with children in their arms,
With doleful cries ran to the farms.

With all their firing and their skill,
They did not any person kill,
Neither was any person hurt,
Except the Reverend Parson Burt.

And he was not killed by a ball,
As judged by jurors one and all,
But being in a sickly state,
He frightened fell, which proved his fate.

Another truth to you I'll tell,
That you may see they leveled well,
For aiming for to kill the people,
They fired their first shot into a steeple.

They fired low, they fired high,
The women scream, the children cry,
And all their firing and their racket
Shot off the topmast of a packet!

Courtesy of N.Y. Public Library Picture Collection.

Yankee Doodle's Expedition to Rhode Island

France's overt participation in the American Revolution began with the arrival in July 1778 of a fleet under the command of Count Charles-Hector d'Estaing. In August he sailed for Rhode Island to assist General John Sullivan in an attempt to dislodge the British from Newport, which they had held since 1776. D'Estaing was met by a British fleet under Lord Howe, and as they prepared to do battle, a storm of such furious violence arose that both fleets were dispersed far and wide. By the time d'Estaing collected his scattered and battered forces, he decided to make for Boston instead of returning to support Sullivan. This fiasco inspired a ditty of derogation to the tune of "Yankee Doodle" that appeared in Rivington's *Royal Gazette* (October 3, 1778).

In the text, "Lewis" is Louis XVI of France; "Monsieur Gérard" is Conrad Alexandre Gérard, the first French minister to the United States, who arrived with d'Estaing; "bold Pigot" is Sir Robert Pigot, the British commander in chief for Rhode Island; "Jonathan" (also "Brother Jonathan") was a nickname or symbol, first for Yankees, then for all Americans. It is said to have originated during the Revolution when General Washington referred to his friend Governor Jonathan Trumbull of Connecticut as "Brother Jonathan." "Jonathan" continued to symbolize America until the early 19th century, when he was replaced by "Uncle Sam."

Rhode Island

From Lew–is, Mon–sieur Gér–ard came, to Con–gress in this town, sir. They bowed to him, and he to them, And then they all sat down, sir. "Be–gar," said Mon–sieur, "One grand *coup*[1] you shall *bien– tôt*[2] be–hold, sir." This

[1]blow
[2]soon

was be—lieved as Gos—pel true, And Jon—a—than felt bold, sir.

So Yankee Doodle did forget
The sound of British drums, sir,
How oft it made him quake and sweat
In spite of Yankee rum, sir.
He took his wallet on his back,
His rifle on his shoulder,
And vowed Rhode Island to attack
Before he was much older.

In dread array, their tattered crew
Advanced with colours spread, sir,
Their fifes played Yankee-doodle-doo,
King Hancock at their head, sir.
What numbers bravely crossed the seas,
I cannot well determine,
A swarm of rebels and of fleas,
And every other vermin.

Their mighty hearts might shrink, they thought,
For all flesh only grass is,
A piteous store they therefore brought
Of whiskey and molasses.
They swore they'd make bold Pigot squeak,
So did their good ally, sir,
And take him pris'ner in a week,
But that was all my eye, sir.

As Jonathan so much desired
To shine in martial story,
D'Estaing with *politesse* retired,
To leave him all the glory.
He left him what was better yet,
At least it was more use, sir,
He left him for a quick retreat,
A very good excuse, sir.

To stay unless he ruled the sea,
He thought would not be right, sir.
And Continental troops, said he,
On islands should not fight, sir.
Another cause with these combined,
To throw him in the dumps, sir,
For Clinton's name alarmed his mind
And made him stir his stumps, sir.

Newport, Rhode Island, 1781. Courtesy of N.Y. Public Library Picture Collection.

The Riflemen of Bennington

In August 1777, British General John Burgoyne put his "grand strategy" into operation. His army, which was grouped around Montreal, would descend into New York and link up in Albany with General Howe's forces marching north from New York City. This would give him control of the Hudson River and effectively divide the Colonies in two. It might well have ended the war then and there if it were not for the unexpectedly successful resistance of the Americans. On August 13, Hessian Lieutenant Colonel Frederick Baume was dispatched by Burgoyne to forage for supplies in Vermont. This incursion resulted in the Battle of Bennington, which ended disastrously for the Hessians.

Vermont

Why come ye hith - er red - coats, your __ minds, what mad – ness fills? There is

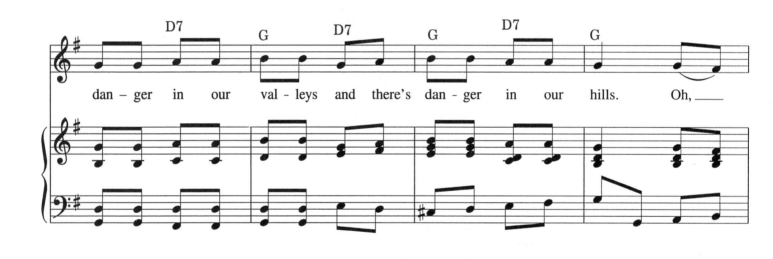

dan – ger in our val – leys and there's dan - ger in our hills. Oh, ____

hear ye not the sing – ing of the bu – gle wild and free? Full ____

Ye ride a goodly steed, ye may know another master,
Ye forward come with speed, but ye'll learn to back much faster
When you meet our mountain boys and their leader Johnny Stark
Lads who make but little noise, lads who always hit the mark. *Chorus*

Had ye no graves at home, across the briny water,
That hither ye must come, like bullocks to the slaughter?
Well, if we work must do, why, the sooner 'tis begun,
If flint and powder hold but true, the sooner 'twill be done. *Chorus*

Calvin Coolidge. Courtesy of N.Y. Public Library Picture Collection.

Keep Cool and Keep Coolidge

Calvin Coolidge, the 30th President of the United States, was the original "Yankee Doodle Dandy." He was born on July 4, 1872, at Plymouth, Vermont. He had been vice president in the administration of the previous President, Warren Harding. When Harding died in office on August 23, 1923, Coolidge succeeded to the presidency, taking the oath of office from his own father, a notary public, in Plymouth.

Vermont

Words by Ida Cheever Goodwin
Music by Bruce Harper

four. He's been tried, he's nev-er want-ing, He is giv-ing of his

best. "Keep cool, and keep Cool-idge," is our coun-try's might-y test.

With a private life of virtue and a public record clean,
He stands upon the summits with a countenance serene,
Defender of the righteous and a juggernaut to wrong,
We'll make him stay in Washington - a hundred million strong. *Chorus*

Mid-Atlantic

Mid-Atlantic

Philadelphia, Pennsylvania, Before 1754. Courtesy of N.Y. Public Library Picture Collection.

The Battle of Trenton

On Christmas morning, 1776, Washington's ragged rebel army rowed across the icy Delaware River and fell upon the 1,200-man Hessian force in Trenton sleeping off its Christmas celebration. It was a much-needed victory, coming after a long series of military reverses for Washington and his men.

New Jersey

On Christ – mas day in sev-en-ty six, Our rag – ged troops with bay-o-nets fixed, For Tren – ton marched a – way. The Del-a-ware see!___ the boats be-low! The light ob-scured___ by hail and snow! But no signs of dis – may.

Our object was the Hessian band,
That dared invade fair freedom's land,
  And quarter in that place.
Great Washington he led us on,
Whose streaming flag in storm or sun,
  Had never known diagrace.

In silent march we passed the night,
Each soldier panting for the fight,
  Though quite benumbed with frost.
Greene, on the left, at six began,
The right was led by Sullivan,
  Who ne'er a moment lost.

Their pickets stormed, the alarm was spread,
That rebels risen from the dead
  Were marching into town.
Some scampered here, some scampered there,
And some for action did prepare;
  But soon their arms laid down.

Twelve hundred servile miscreants,
With all their colors, guns and tents,
  Were trophies of the day.
The frolic o'er, the bright canteen,
In center, front and rear was seen
  Driving fatigue away.

Now, brothers of the patriot bands,
Let's sing deliverance from the hands
  Of arbitrary sway.
And as our life is but a span,
Let's touch the tankard while we can,
  In memory of that day.

The Old Barracks
ERECTED 1758
OPEN DAILY
CLOSED SUNDAYS   ADMISSION 10¢

Trenton, New Jersey. Courtesy of N.Y. Public Library Picture Collection.

Song of the Minute Man

Major General Benjamin Lincoln's revolutionary army was stationed near Bound Brook in their winter quarters in 1777. Seven miles away, in New Brunswick, was the encampment of the British and Hessian troops. In April the Americans were attacked in a memorable engagement. The New Jersey militiaman who wrote this song used the term "Minute Man," which at the time was applied to many state militias — not only to the Minute Men of Massachusetts, who were the first to be so called.

New Jersey

Come_ rise up broth–er Min–ute Men and let us have_ a_ cho – rus, The_
brav–er and the bol – der, the more they will a – dore us. Our_
coun–try calls for swords and balls, and drums a – loud doth rat – tle. Our_
fif–er's charms a – rise to arms and Lib–er–ty calls to_ bat – tle.

We have some noble congressmen elected for our nurses,
And every jolly farmer will assist us with their purses;
We let them stay at home, we say, enjoy their wives with pleasure,
And we will go and fight our foes and save their lives and treasure.

Now to our station, let us march, and rendezvous with pleasure,
We have been like brave Minute Men to serve so great a treasure;
We let them see immediately that we are men of mettle,
We Jersey boys that fear no noise will never flinch for battle.

And when we do return again, it will be with glory,
For them that do remain at home to hear a valiant story;
They will draw near and be glad to hear, no doubting of the wonder,
That Minute Men, though one to ten, should bring the Tories under.

So let us not be dismayed although the Tories thunder,
They only want to ruin us and live upon our plunder.
Our cause is just, therefore we must withstand all their boodle,
If they advance, we will make them dance the tune of Yankee Doodle.

Battle of Camden. Courtesy of N.Y. Public Library Picture Collection.

The Bombing of Lewes-1813

Poet Gilbert Byron has devoted his literary life to documenting the people, the places, and the events that make up the fabric of his native Delaware.

Words by Gilbert Byron
Music by Jerry Silverman

Delaware

During the war of eight-een twelve, A Brit-ish fleet sailed in ___ the ___ bay, Trained its guns on old Lew-es town, Gave the peo-ple just one day To furn-ish twen-ty bul-locks, fat, ___ Man-y hogs-heads of wa-ter, sweet. Eith-er yield to the king's re-quest, ___ Or to the guns of the Brit-ish fleet.

in our day. And just to add my lit – tle _ i – ron, The Brit-ish com – man – der's name was By-ron.

Colonel Samuel Davis answered, "No!"
He'd never feed a British mouth,
And trained his little twelve pounders
Toward the big fleet in the south.
With that the British fleet opened up,
Two hundred and forty cannon boomed,
Solid lead screamed overhead,
Fire rockets whistled, scrapnel zoomed,

But their aim was so atrocious,
After twenty-two hours of this squeeze,
A hound dog and a setting hen
Were the only casualties.
While the citizens picked solid ball
From the streets like manna bread,
And the little guns of Lewes
Gave the British back their lead.

And when British marines tried to land
The citizens turned them back,
Old men paraded with cornstalks,
British eyes were fooled by that.
They raised their sails so silently,
Slipped out of the Delaware Bay
And they never came back again,
At least not in our day.

And just to add my little iron,
The British commander's name was Byron.

Small Wonder

Truth, Delawareans are an inert lot. Most of them live with their parents until they are 35 and eat hoagies three times a day. There's an inherent inferiority complex too, since after all, we're the second (and only the second) smallest state. That's why, when I wrote "Small Wonder," I was glad I could come up with something good to say. We are unique, not in our natural wonders or our creativity; but there is a Delaware attitude, good or bad. The earliest founders were Dutch and Swiss, with Quakers soon after up North. Tight folks. (Jerry "Crabmeat" Thompson)

Delaware

By Jerry "Crabmeat" Thompson

Small won-der, small it's true, Small won-der, I love you.

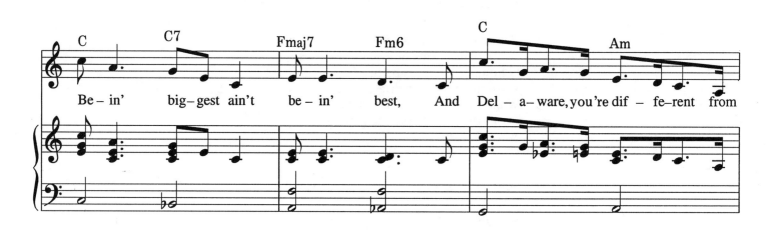

Be-in' big-gest ain't be-in' best, And Del-a-ware, you're dif-fe-rent from

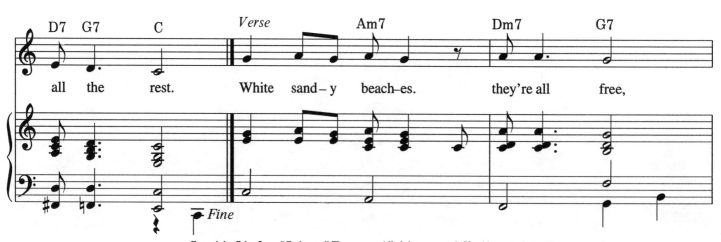

all the rest. White sand-y beach-es. they're all free,

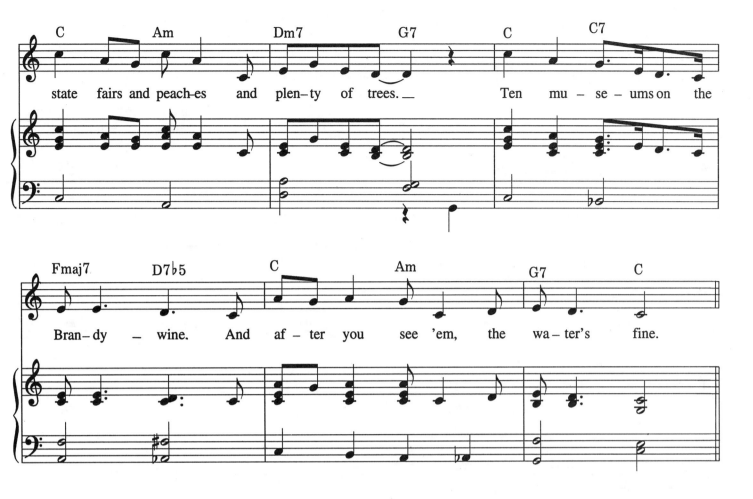

state fairs and peach-es and plen-ty of trees.__ Ten mu - se - ums on the

Bran-dy __ wine. And af - ter you see 'em, the wa-ter's fine.

Caesar Rodney was one of our greats,
His race to Philly made us the First State.
Now Richard Pett's at the Dover track,
And Caesar's a statue with pigeons on his hat. *Chorus*

We're the home of the Du Pont Company,
Blue Hen football and the wing-T.
George Thorogood, the Phanatic and Music Loop Night,
And Dewey Beach–A WAY OF LIFE. *Chorus*

So, come see Delaware and make sure
Not to miss the famous furniture at Winterthur.
There's history galore, and four race tracks,
So get here quick, 'cus there's no sales tax! *Chorus*

Tell you how to get here–it won't take long;
We're across the river from Jersey, like in the song.
We're next to Philadelphia, and Mary Land too,
And the Chesapeake Canal cuts us right in two. *Chorus*

All the folks back home would sure be sickened,
If I forgot to mention our friends the chickens;
The Fighting Blue Hen is our state fowl,
And they pretty much run things below the canal. *Chorus*

Wilmington, Delaware. Courtesy of N.Y. Public Library Picture Collection.

41

Maryland, My Maryland

James R. Randall, who wrote the lyrics to this song on April 23, 1861, hoped that his poem would inspire Maryland to join the Confederacy. Despite its great popularity, Maryland did not secede.

Words by James R. Randall
Music: "Tannenbaum"

Maryland

queen of yore,   Ma – ry– land,   my   Ma – ry – land!

Hark to an exiled son's appeal,
  Maryland, my Maryland!
My Mother State, to thee I kneel,
  Maryland, my Maryland!
For life or death, for woe or weal,
Thy peerless chivalry reveal,
And gird thy beauteous limbs with steel,
  Maryland, my Maryland!

Thou wilt not cower in the dust,
  Maryland, my Maryland!
Thy beaming sword shall never rust,
  Maryland, my Maryland!
Remember Carroll's sacred trust,
Remember Howard's warlike thrust,
And all thy slumberers with the just,
  Maryland, my Maryland!

Come! 'tis the red dawn of the day,
  Maryland, my Maryland!
Come! with thy panoplied array,
  Maryland, my Maryland!
With Ringgold's spirit for the fray,
With Watson's blood at Monterey,
With fearless Lowe and dashing May,
  Maryland, my Maryland!

Dear mother, burst the tyrant's chain,
  Maryland, my Maryland!
Virginia should not call in vain,
  Maryland, my Maryland!
She meets her sisters on the plain,
"Sic temper!" 'tis the proud refrain
That baffles minions back amain,
  Maryland, my Maryland!
Arise in majesty again,   ⎤
  Maryland, my Maryland!   ⎦ *Repeat last 4 measures*

The Post Office, Baltimore, Maryland. Courtesy of N.Y. Public Library Picture Collection.

Baltimore Fire

On February 7 and 8, 1904, a tremendous fire wiped out practically the entire downtown section of Baltimore. Jones Falls, referred to in this song as "silver falls," was one of the points at which the fire-fighters stopped the advance of the blaze.

one sad cry of__ pi—ty.__   Bal—ti—more, the beau—ti ful   cit-y.__
ru – in laid Fair_____

Amid an awful struggle of commotion,
The wind blew a gale from the ocean.
Brave firemen struggled with devotion,
But their gallant efforts they all proved in vain.   *Chorus*

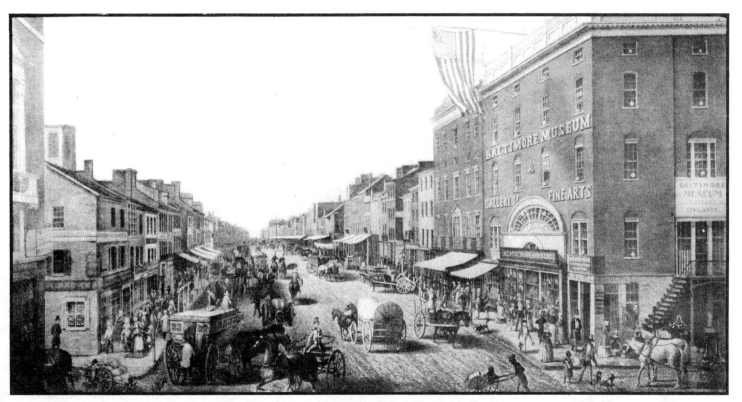

Old Baltimore in Stage-Coach Days. Courtesy of N.Y. Public Library Picture Collection.

The Battle of Saratoga

American General Horatio Gates' victory over Burgoyne at Saratoga on October 17, 1777, brought the British plan (described in "The Riflemen of Bennington") to a disastrous end. This long ballad typically mentions many names which would have been familiar to contemporary listeners: St. Clair (American Major General Arthur St. Clair), Herkimer (General Nicholas Herkimer of the New York militia, fatally wounded in the battle of Oriskany, August 6, 1777), Sellinger (actually British Lieutenant Colonel Barry St. Leger), Brooks (Colonel John Brooks of the Massachusetts militia), Arnold (Brigadier General Benedict Arnold, who in 1780 attempted to betray the American fort at West Point to the British), Baume (Lt. Colonel Frederick Baume, whose ill-fated exploits are recounted in "The Riflemen of Bennington"), Stark (Brigadier General John Stark, victor over Baume at Bennington), and Lincoln (American General Benjamin Lincoln, who played a key role in the Battle of Saratoga).

New York

Come un–to me ye he – roes whose hearts are true and bold, _____ Who

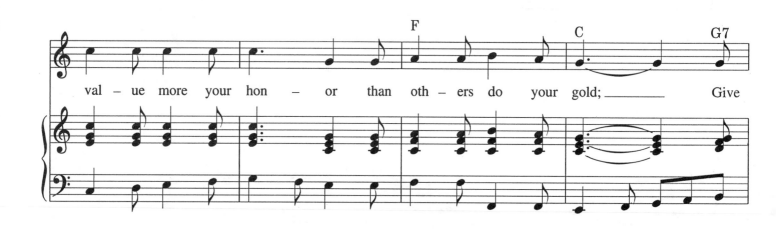

val – ue more your hon – or than oth–ers do your gold; _____ Give

ear un–to my sto – ry and I the truth will tell, _____ Con–

Burgoyne, the king's commander, from Canada set sail,
With full eight thousand reg'lars, he thought he could not fail;
With Indians and Canadians and his curséd Tory crew,
On board his fleet of shipping, he up the Champlain flew.
    He up the Champlain flew, he up the Champlain flew,
    On board his fleet of shipping, he up the Champlain flew.

Before Ticonderoga, the first day of July,
Appeared his ships and army, and we did them espy.
Their motions we observed full well both night and day,
And our brave boys prepared to have a bloody fray.
    To have a bloody fray, etc.

Our garrison they viewed then, and straight their troops did land,
And when St. Clair, our chieftain, the fact did understand,
That they the Mount Defiance were bent to fortify,
He found we must surrender or else prepare to die.
    Or else prepare to die, etc.

The fifth day of July, then, he ordered a retreat,
And when next morn we started, Burgoyne thought we were beat.
And closely he pursued us, till when near Hubbardton
Our rear guards were defeated, he thought the country won.
  He thought the country won, etc.

And when 'twas told in Congress that we our forts had left,
To Albany retreated, of all the north bereft;
Brave General Gates they sent us, our fortunes to retrieve,
And him with shouts of gladness, the army did receive.
  The army did receive, etc.

Where first the Mohawk's waters do in the sunshine play,
For Herkimer's brave soldiers, Sellinger ambushed lay;
And them he there defeated, but soon he had his due,
And scared by Brooks and Arnold, he to the north withdrew.

To take the stores and cattle that we had gathered then,
Burgoyne sent a detachment of fifteen hundred men;
By Baum they were commanded, to Bennington they went;
To plunder and to murder was fully their intent.

But little did they know then with whom they had to deal,
It was not quite so easy our stores and stock to steal;
Bold Stark would give them only a portion of his lead;
With half his crew 'ere sunset, Baum lay among the dead.

The nineteenth of September, the morning cool and clear,
Brave Gates rode through our army, each soldier's heart to cheer;
"Burgoyne," he cried, "advances, but we will never fly;
No, rather than surrender, we'll fight him till we die."

The news was quickly brought us the enemy was near,
And all along our lines then there was no sign of fear;
It was above Stillwater we met at noon that day,
And everyone expected to see a bloody fray.

Six hours the battle lasted, each heart was true as gold,
The British fought like lions, and we like Yankees bold;
The leaves with blood were crimson, and then brave Gates did cry,
"'Tis diamond now cut diamond! We'll beat them, boys, or die."

The darkness soon approaching, it forced us to retreat
Into our lines till morning, which made them think us beat;
But 'ere the sun was risen, they saw before their eyes,
Us ready to engage them, which did them much surprise.

Of fighting they seem weary, therefore to work they go,
Their thousand dead to bury and breastworks up to throw;
With grape and bombs intending our army to destroy,
Or from our works our forces by stratagem decoy.

The seventh day of October, the British tried again,
Shells from their cannon throwing, which fell on us like rain;
To drive us from our stations, that they might thus retreat;
For now Burgoyne saw plainly, he never could us beat.

But vain was his endeavor our men to terrify;
Though death was all around us, not one of us would fly.
But when an hour we'd fought them and they began to yield,
Along our lines the cry ran, "The next blow wins the field!"

Great God, who guides their battles, whose cause is just and true,
Inspire our bold commander, the course he should pursue.
He ordered Arnold forward and Brooks to follow on;
The enemy was routed, our liberty was won!

Then burning all their luggage, they fled with haste and fear,
Burgoyne with all his forces, to Saratoga did steer;
And Gates, our brave commander, soon after him did hie,
Resolving he would take them or in the effort die.

As we came nigh the village, we overtook the foe,
They'd burned each house to ashes, like all where'er they go.
The seventeenth of October, they did capitulate,
Burgoyne and his proud army did we our pris'ners make.

Now, here's a health to Arnold and our commander Gates,
To Lincoln and to Washington, whom every Tory hates;
Likewise unto our Congress, God grant it long to reign;
Our country, Right and Justice forever to maintain.

Now finished is my story, my song is at an end;
The freedom we're enjoying we're ready to defend;
For while our cause is righteous, heaven nerves the soldier's arm,
And vain is their endeavor who strive to do us harm.

Battle of Saratoga. Courtesy of N.Y. Public Library Picture Collection.

Low Bridge!-Everybody Down

(Fifteen Years on the Erie Canal)

Twenty years after New York Governor De Witt Clinton floated down the newly opened Erie Canal on the *Sequoia Chief* from Buffalo to Albany and down the Hudson River to New York harbor in 1825, Michigan had increased its population by 60 times and Ohio had climbed from 13th to the 3rd most heavily populated state in the Union. The Erie Canal was the highway for most of these settlers and their goods. Clinton's 425-mile ditch had proved itself. New York was, indeed, the Empire State.

By Thomas S. Allen
(1913)

New York

50

We better be on our way old pal,
Fifteen years on the Erie Canal.
'Cause you bet your life I'd never part from Sal,
Fifteen years on the Erie Canal.
Get up there, mule, here comes a lock,
We'll make Rome 'bout six o'clock.
One more trip and back we'll go,
Right back home to Buffalo. *Chorus*

I don't have to call when I want my Sal,
Fifteen years on the Erie Canal;
She trots from her stall like a good old gal.
Fifteen years on the Erie Canal,
I eat my meals with Sal each day,
I eat beef and she eats hay,
She ain't so slow if you want to know,
She put the "Buff" in Buffalo. *Chorus*

51

The Battle of the Kegs

In January 1778, a British fleet lay at anchor in the Delaware River off Philadelphia. American patriot David Bushnell, the inventor of the submarine, hit upon the idea of floating explosive mines in the form of kegs of gunpowder down the river into the very heart of the fleet. One keg actually exploded when a barge crew attempted to fish that strange object from the water. When other kegs appeared floating toward the ships, the British opened fire on them with everything they had. Although Bushnell's ingenious plan ultimately failed, the panic and consternation demonstrated by the British caused great amusement among the Yankees. Francis Hopkinson, a member of the Continental Congress from New Jersey and signer of the Declaration of Independence, seized upon this incident to compose this ballad, which was sung with great delight by one and all.

Pennsylvania

Words by Francis Hopkinson

Gal – lants, at – tend, and hear a friend Trill forth har – mon–ious dit – ty, Strange things I'll tell which late be – fell in Phil – a – del – phia Cit – y. 'Twas ear – ly day, as po – ets say, Just when the sun was ris – ing, A

sol – dier stood on log of wood, And saw a sight sur – pris – ing.

As, in amaze, he stood to gaze;
The truth can't be denied, sirs,
He spied a score of kegs – or more,
Come floating down the tide, sirs.
A sailor, too, in jerkin blue,
The strange appearance viewing,
First damned his eyes in great surprise,
Then said, "Some mischief brewing.

"The kegs now hold the rebel bold
Packed up like pickled herring;
And they've come down to attack the town
In this new way of ferrying."
The soldier flew, the sailor, too,
And, scared almost to death, sirs,
Wore out their shoes to spread the news,
And ran till out of breath, sirs.

Now up and down, throughout the town,
Most frantic scenes were acted;
And some ran here and some ran there,
Like men almost distracted,
Some "fire" cried, which some denied,
But said the earth had quakéd;
And girls and boys, with hideous noise,
Ran through the town half-naked.

Sir William, he, snug as a flea,
Lay all this time a-snoring,
Nor dreamed of harm, as he lay warm
In bed with Mrs. Loring.
Now in a fright, he starts upright,
Awaked by such a clatter;
He rubs both eyes and boldly cried,
"For God's sake, what's the matter?"

At his bedside he then espied
Sir Erskine at command, sirs;
Upon one foot he had a boot,
And t'other in his hand, sirs,
"Arise! Arise!" Sir Erskine cries;
"The rebels – more's the pity
Without a boat are all afloat,
And ranged before the city.

"The motley crew, in vessels new
With Satan for their guide, sir,
Packed up in bags, or wooden kegs,
Come driving down the tide, sir.
Therefore, prepare for bloody war!
Those kegs must all be routed,
Or surely we despised shall be,
And British courage doubted."

The royal band now ready stand,
All ranged in dead array, sirs,
With stomach stout to see it out,
And make a bloody day, sirs.
The cannons roar from shore to shore,
The small arms make a rattle;
Since wars began, I'm sure no man
E'er saw so strange a battle.

The rebel vales, the rebel dales,
With rebel trees surrounded,
The distant woods, the hills and floods,
With rebel echoes sounded.
The fish below swam to and fro,
Attacked from every quarter;
"Why, sure," thought they, "the devil's to pay
'Mongst folks above the water."

The kegs, 'tis said, tho' strongly made
Of rebel staves and hoops, sirs,
Could not oppose the powerful foes,
The conquering British troops, sirs.
From morn to night these men of might
Displayed amazing courage,
And when the sun was fairly down
Returned to sup their porridge.

A hundred men, with each a pen,
Or more – upon my words, sirs,
It is most true – would be too few
Their valor to record, sirs,
Such feats did they perform that day
Upon those wicked kegs, sirs,
That years to come, if they get home,
They'll make their boasts and brags, sirs.

The Johnstown Flood

On May 31, 1889, "the worst peacetime disaster of the nation's history" took place when the South Fork Dam, 400 feet above and 16 miles beyond Johnstown, broke. It sent a roaring 40-foot wall of water rushing down upon the hapless city with unbelievable destructive force. Everything in its path was destroyed. When the waters subsided, a tremendous fire broke out, which added to the misery and destruction. The flood left 35,000 people homeless and 2,200 dead.

Pennsylvania

On a bal–my day in May, When na–ture held full sway, And the birds sang sweet–ly in the sky a–bove; A cit–y lay se–rene, In a val–ley deep and green, Where thou–sands dwelt in hap–pi–ness and love.

Chorus

Now the cry of dis – tress rings from east to the west, And our whole dear coun – try now is plunged in woe. For the thous – ands burned and drowned in the cit – y of Johns – town, All were lost in that great o – ver – flow.

Ah! but soon the scene was changed;
For just like a thing deranged,
A storm came crashing thru the quiet town;
Now the wind it raved and shrieked,
Thunder rolled and lightning streaked;
But the rain it poured in awful torrents down.   *Chorus*

Like the Paul Revere of old
Came a rider brave and bold;
On a big horse he was flying like a deer;
And he shouted warning shrill,
"Quickly fly off to the hills."
But the people smiled and showed no signs of fear.   *Chorus*

Ah! but e'er he turned away
This brave rider and the bay
And the many thousand souls he tried to save;
But they had no time to spare,
Nor to offer up a prayer,
Now they were hurried off into a watery grave.   *Chorus*

Fathers, mothers, children all
Both the young, old, great, and small
They were thrown about like chaff before the wind;
When the fearful raging flood
Rushing where city stood,
Leaving thousands dead and dying there behind.   *Chorus*

Now the cry of fire arose
Like the screams of battling foes,
For that dreadful sick'ning pile was now on fire;
As they poured out prayers to heaven
They were burned as in an oven,
And that dreadful pile formed their funeral pyre.   *Chorus*

Lower Half of Johnstown a Few Months After the Flood. Courtesy of N.Y. Public Library Picture Collection.

56

Appalachian Highlands

Highlands

Irvington, Kentucky, 1938. Courtesy of N.Y. Public Library Picture Collection.

The Hunters of Kentucky

Frontier "bragging" was very much an accepted form of expression. Andrew Jackson's Kentucky riflemen let it be known that they were "half horse — half alligator." This song details their exploits at the Battle of New Orleans (January 8, 1815). It was used as a campaign song for Jackson in the presidential election of 1824. See the song "The Battle of New Orleans" for further details concerning this memorable engagement.

Kentucky

Words by Samuel Woodword
Music: "Unfortunate Miss Bailey"

Ye gen-tle-men and la-dies fair, Who grace this fa-mous cit-y, Just lis-ten if you've time to spare, While I re-hearse a dit-ty; And for the op-por-tu-ni-ty con-ceive your-selves quite luck-y, For 'tis not of-ten that you see a hunt-er from Ken-tuck-y.

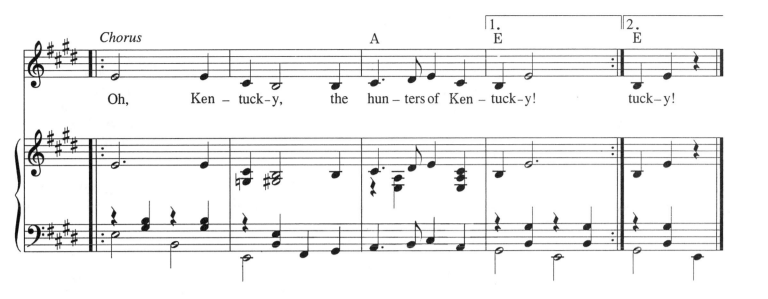

Chorus

Oh, Ken-tuck-y, the hun-ters of Ken-tuck-y! tuck-y!

We are a hardy, free-born race,
  Each man to fear a stranger;
Whate'er the game we join in chase,
  Despoiling time and danger,
And if a daring foe annoys,
  Whate'er his strength and forces,
We'll show him that Kentucky boys
  Are alligator horses. *Chorus*

I s'pose you've read it in the prints,
  How Packenham attempted
To make old Hickory Jackson wince,
  But soon his scheme repented;
For we, with rifles ready cock'd,
  Thought such occasion lucky,
And soon around the gen'ral flock'd
  The hunters of Kentucky. *Chorus*

You've heard, I s'pose how New Orleans
  Is fam'd for wealth and beauty,
There's girls of ev'ry hue it seems,
  From snowy white to sooty.
So Packenham he made his brags,
  If he in fight was lucky,
He'd have their girls and cotton bags,
  In spite of old Kentucky. *Chorus*

But Jackson he was wide awake,
  And was not scar'd at trifles,
For well he knew what aim we take
  With our Kentucky rifles.
He led us down to Cypress swamp,
  The ground was low and mucky,
There stood John Bull in martial pomp
  And here was old Kentucky. *Chorus*

A bank was rais'd to hide our breasts,
  Not that we thought of dying,
But that we always like to rest,
  Unless the game is flying.
Behind it stood our little force,
  None wished it to be greater,
For ev'ry man was half a horse,
  And half an alligator. *Chorus*

They did not let our patience tire,
  Before they show'd their faces;
We did not choose to waste our fire,
  So snugly kept our places.
But when so near we saw them wink,
  We thought it time to stop 'em,
And 'twould have done you good I think,
  To see Kentuckians drop 'em. *Chorus*

They found, at last, 'twas vain to fight,
  Where lead was all the booty,
And so they wisely took to flight,
  And left us all our beauty.
And now, if danger e'er annoys,
  Remember what our trade is,
Just send for us Kentucky boys,
  And we'll protect ye, ladies. *Chorus*

Sixteen Tons

I was raised in the southwestern coal fields of Kentucky. My father was a miner in the little town of Beech Creek in Muhlenberg County.... Then there were the strikes! To us and all the people we knew, it meant "Root, hog, or die." I became well acquainted with the "aid-hall." There we'd go to get whatever was to be given in the way of food to miners on strike. Just enough beans and salt pork to keep body and soul together.... The promise of miners becoming united was music to the ears of the miners and their wives, but the entertainment they'd have between speeches was more musical to my young ears. (Merle Travis, whose unique virtuoso style of guitar playing has come to be known as "Travis picking.")

Kentucky

By Merle Travis

Some folks say a man's made out of mud,___ But a poor man's made out of

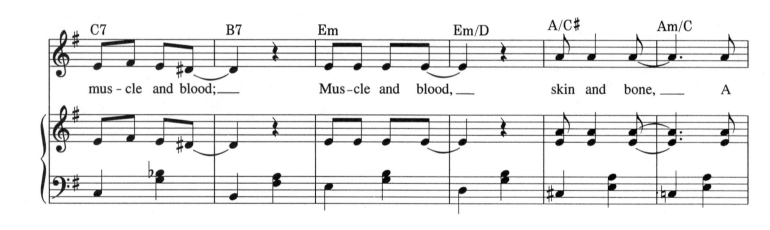

mus-cle and blood;___ Mus-cle and blood, ___ skin and bone, ___ A

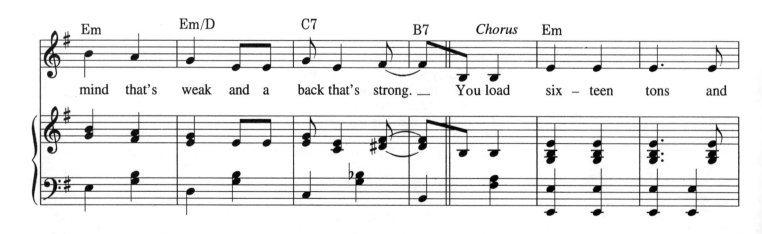

mind that's weak and a back that's strong. __ You load six – teen tons and

what do you get, ____ but an—oth—er day old — er and deep—er in debt. ____

____ Saint Pet—er, don't you call me, 'cause I can't go — I owe my

soul to the com—pa—ny store.

I was born one morning when the sun didn't shine,
I picked up my shovel and I walked to the mine,
Loaded sixteen ton of Number Nine coal,
And the straw boss hollered, "Well, bless my soul!"   *Chorus*

I was born one morning in a drizzling rain,
Fighting and trouble is my middle name.
I was raised in the bottom by a mama hound,
I'm mean as a dog but I'm as gentle as a lamb.   *Chorus*

If you see me coming, better step aside,
A lot of men didn't and a lot of me died;
I got a fist of iron and a fist of steel,
If the right one don't get you then the left one will.   *Chorus*

61

Chief Aderholt

*The 1929 strike at the Loray mills in Gastonia, North Carolina, began like hundreds of others in the southern textile industry, but ended as the South's greatest labor trial.... The story of the strike...a mill community, exploited, oppressed, discouraged, and sullen in its discouragement, is aroused to action by Northern organizers.... The strike dragged on through the summer months, and the mill owners turned the strikers out of the company-owned houses. The evicted workers set up a tent colony on the edge of town...the strikers formed a picket line...and prepared to march to the mill a mile away, where the night shift still carried on operations. They had gone only a short distance when a band of deputy sheriffs and police attacked them.... One of the officers then fired at the strikers' headquarters, and the answering shots killed O. F. Aderholt, Gastonia police chief. (*American Folksongs of Protest* by John Greenway, 1953)*

Ella May Wiggins, who had worked in a textile mill 60 hours a week for ten years as a spinner, found her voice as a singing union song writer. She herself was shot to death on the way to a union meeting in Gastonia on September 14, 1929. In this song, Vera is Vera Buch, one of the union organizers. Manville Jenckes was the owner of the Loray mill.

North Carolina   **By Ella May Wiggins**

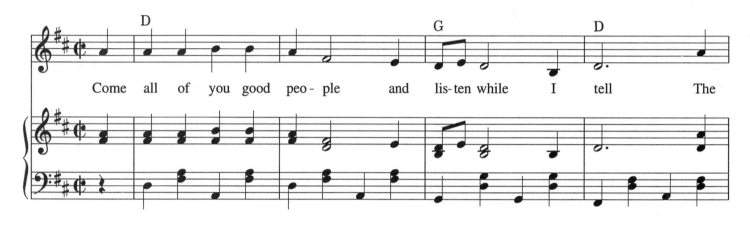

Come all of you good peo-ple and lis-ten while I tell The

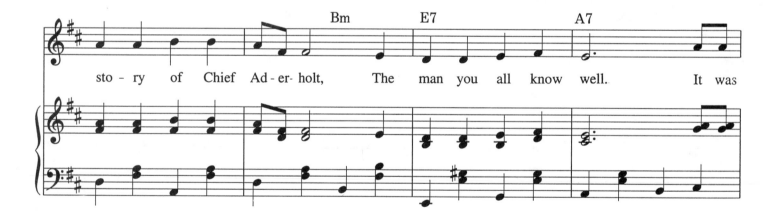

sto-ry of Chief Ad-er-holt, The man you all know well. It was

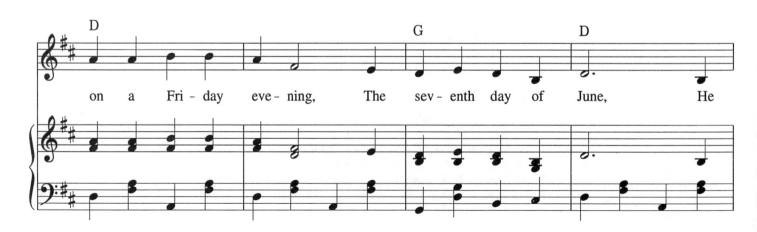

on a Fri-day eve-ning, The sev-enth day of June, He

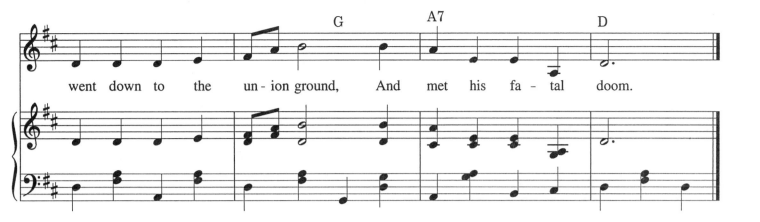

went down to the un-ion ground, And met his fa-tal doom.

They locked up our leaders, they put them into jail,
They shoved them into prison, refused to give them bail.
The workers joined together, and this was their reply,
"We'll never, no, we'll never, let our leaders die."

They moved the trial to Charlotte, got lawyers from every town;
I'm sure we'll hear them speak again upon the union ground.
While Vera, she's in prison, Manville Jenckes is in pain.
Come join the Textile Union, and show them you are game.

We're going to have a union over the South,
Where we can wear good clothes, and live in a better house;
No we must stand together, and to the boss reply,
"We'll never, no, we'll never, let our leaders die."

Tobacco Worker Near Durham, North Carolina, 1940. Courtesy of N.Y. Public Library Picture Collection.

Swannanoa Tunnel

The Swannanoa Tunnel goes through the Blue Ridge Mountains 20 miles from Asheville. It was completed around 1883 with the help of Negro convicts.

North Carolina

I'm goin' back to Swannanoa Tunnel,
That's my home, honey, that's my home.

When you hear that hoot owl squallin',
Somebody's dyin', honey, somebody's dyin'.

When you hear that pistol growl, baby,
Another man's gone – another man's gone.

If I could gamble like Tom Dooley
I'd leave my home, honey, I'd leave my home.

Jimmy Polk of Tennessee

James K. Polk (1795–1849) was the 11th President of the United States. He defeated Henry Clay in the election of 1844, having beaten out Martin Van Buren ("Matty Van") and James Buchanan for the Democratic nomination. The "Locofocoes" were a radical wing of the Democratic party, whose name derived from a recent invention: a type of self-illuminating safety match.

Words by J. Greinerl
Music: "Dandy Jim of Caroline"

Tennessee

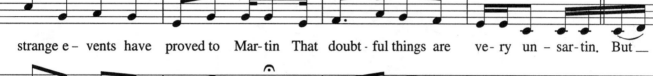

Oh, ev-'ry day brings some-thing new, The Lo-co-fo-coes find it so; And

strange e-vents have proved to Mar-tin That doubt-ful things are ve-ry un-sar-tin. But __

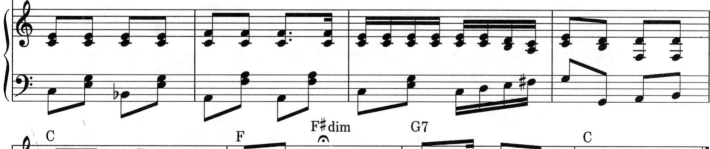

hark, the peop-le ris-ing say, That he is not the man to cope with Hen-ry Clay, Ha,

ha, ha, ha, Such a nom-i-nee, As Jim-my Polk of Ten-nes-see.

65

Come listen Whigs and Locos all,
Your kind attention here I call,
And mark the burthen of the glee,
Ex-Speaker Polk of Tennessee.   *Chorus*

Polk's choice occasioned some surprise,
Good Democrats rolled up their eyes,
Our candidate, pray, who is he?
Why James K. Polk of Tennessee.   *Chorus*

But soon their vast excitement o'er,
They see what ne'er was seen before,
The best selection that could be,
Ex-Speaker Polk of Tennessee.   *Chorus*

Fall down before a better man,
Than even little Matty Van,
Buchanan too, must bow the knee
To Ex-Speaker Polk of Tennessee.   *Chorus*

James Knox Polk. Courtesy of N.Y. Public Library Picture Collection.

Buddy Won't You Roll Down The Line?

In the 1880s, southern miners tried to organize the Knights of Labor. In Tennessee their efforts were thwarted by the presence in the mines of thousands of convicts, leased at $60 a head by the state government to the coal companies.

Tennessee

Way back yon-der in Ten - nes - see they leased the
la - bor fought___ a - gainst it, – To win it

con - victs out,___ They put them work - ing
took some time,___ But while the lease was

in the mines a – gainst free la - bor stout. Free
in ef - fect, they

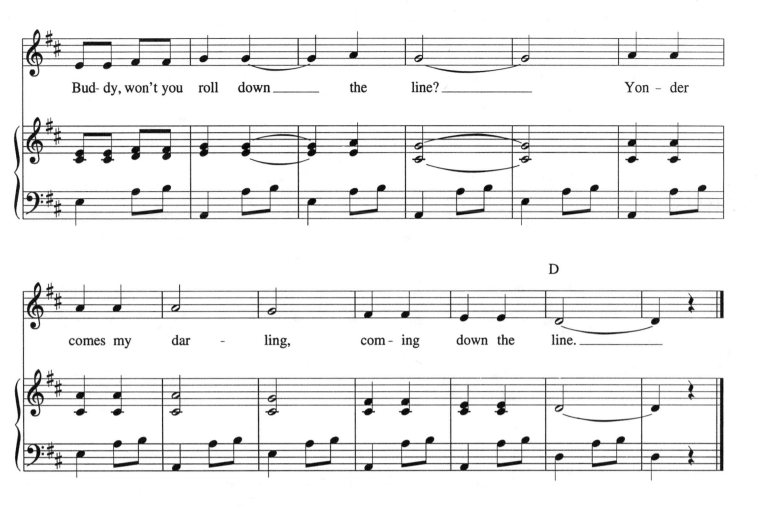

Bud-dy, won't you roll down _____ the line? _____ Yon-der

comes my dar - ling, com - ing down the line. _____

Every Monday morning they get you out on time,
March you down to Lone Rock just to look into that mine.
March you down to Lone Rock to look into that hole,
Very last words the captain say, "You better get your pole." *Chorus*

The beans they are half done, the bread is not so well,
The meat it is all burnt up and the coffee's black as heck,
But when you get your task done, you're glad to come to call,
For anything you get to eat, it tastes good done or raw. *Chorus*

Foster's Mill, Tennessee. Courtesy of N.Y. Public Library Picture Collection.

Richmond Is a Hard Road to Travel

The road to the Confederacy's capital was paved with good intentions and poor military strategy of the Union high command, and Southern rhymesters did not miss any opportunity to celebrate this fact in song. Written in 1863, this lengthy satiric tome was ironically dedicated to Union General Ambrose E. Burnside (whose facial hair style has given us the word "sideburn" JS), and gleefully recounted the travails of his all-too-numerous predecessors. (Songs of the Civil War by Irwin Silber, 1960)

Words: anonymous
Music by Daniel D. Emmett ("Jordan Is a Hard Road to Travel")

Virginia

Would you like to hear my song? I'm a-fraid it's rath-er
'Tis pret-ty hard to sing, and like a round, round

long, Of the fa-mous "On to Rich-mond" dou-ble trou-ble;
ring, 'Tis a dread-ful knot-ty puz-zle to un-rav-el,

Of the half a doz-en trips, and half a doz-en
Though all the pa-pers swore, when we touched Vir-gin-ia's

slips, And the ver - y lat - est burst - ing of the bub - ble?
shore, That Rich-mond was a hard road to trav - el.

Chorus

Then pull off your coat and roll ___ up your sleeve, For

Rich - mond is a hard road to trav - el;   Then

pull off your coat and roll ___ up your sleeve, For

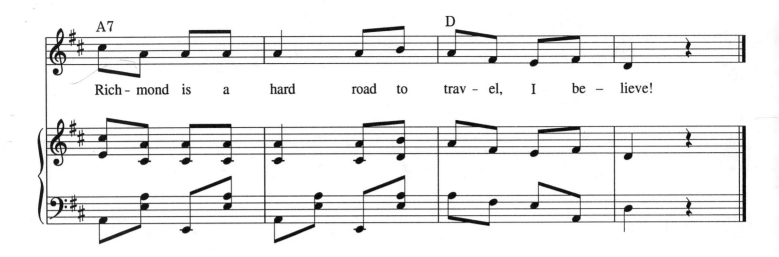

Rich-mond is a hard road to trav-el, I be-lieve!

First, McDowell, bold and gay, set forth the shortest way,
By Manassas in the pleasant summer weather,
But unfortunately ran on a Stonewall, foolish man,
And had a "rocky journey" altogether;
And he found it rather hard to ride o'er Beauregard,
And Johnston proved a deuce of a bother,
And 'twas clear beyond a doubt that he didn't like the route,
And a second time would have to try another.
    Then pull off your coat and roll up your sleeve,
    For Manassas is a hard road to travel;
    Manassas gave us fits, and Bull Run made us grieve,
    For Richmond is a hard road to travel, I believe!

Next came the Wooly-Horse,* with an overwhelming force,
To march down to Richmond by the Valley,
But he couldn't find the road, and his "onward movement" showed
His campaigning was a mere shilly-shally.
Then Commissary Banks, with his motley foreign ranks,
Kicking up a great noise, fuss, and flurry,
Lost the whole of his supplies, and with tears in his eyes,
From the Stonewall ran away in a hurry.
    Then pull off your coat and roll up your sleeve,
    For the Valley is a hard road to travel;
    The Valley wouldn't do and we all had to leave,
    For Richmond is a hard road to travel, I believe!

Then the great *Galena* came, with her portholes all aflame,
And the *Monitor* that famous naval wonder,
But the guns at Drury's Bluff gave them speedily enough,
The loudest sort of reg'lar Rebel thunder.
The *Galena* was astonished and the *Monitor* admonished,
Our patent shot and shell were mocked at,
While the dreadful *Naugatuck,* by the hardest kind of luck,
Was knocked into an ugly cocked hat.
    Then pull off your coat and roll up your sleeve,
    For James River is a hard road to travel;
    The gun-boats gave it up in terror and despair,
    For Richmond is a hard road to travel, I declare!

*General John C. Fremont

Then McClellan followed soon, both with spade and balloon,
To try the Peninsular approaches,
But one and all agreed that his best rate of speed
Was no faster than the slowest of "slow coaches."
Instead of easy ground, at Williamsburg he found
A *Longstreet* indeed, and nothing shorter,
And it put him in the dumps, that spades wasn't trumps,
And the *Hills* he couldn't level "as he orter."
    Then pull off your coat and roll up your sleeve,
    For *Longstreet* is a hard road to travel;
    Lay down the shovel, and throw away the spade,
    For Richmond is a hard road to travel, I'm afraid!

Then said Lincoln unto Pope, "You can make the trip, I hope
I will save the Universal Yankee nation,
To make sure of no defeat, I'll leave no lines of retreat,
And issue a famous proclamation."
But that same dreaded Jackson, this fellow laid his wacks on,
And made him, by compulsion, a *seceder,**
And Pope took rapid flight from Manassas' second fight,
'Twas his very last appearance as a leader.
    Then pull off your coat and roll up your sleeve,
    For *Stonewall* is a hard road to travel;
    Pope did his very best, but was evidently sold,
    For Richmond is a hard road to travel, I am told!

Last of all the brave Burnside, with his pontoon bridges, tried
A road no one had thought of before him,
With two hundred thousand men for the Rebel slaughter pen,
And the blessed Union flag waving o'er him;
But he met a fire like hell, of canister and shell,
That mowed his men down with great slaughter,
'Twas a shocking sight to view, that second Waterloo,
And the river ran with more blood than water.
    Then pull off your coat and roll up your sleeve,
    Rappahannock is a hard road to travel;
    Burnside got in a trap, which caused him for to grieve,
    For Richmond is a hard road to travel, I believe!

We are very much perplexed to know who is the next
To command the new Richmond expedition,
For the Capitol must blaze, and that in ninety days,
And Jeff and his men be sent to perdition.
We'll take the cursed town, and then we'll burn it down,
And plunder and hang up each cursed Rebel;
Yet the contraband was right when he told us they would fight,
"Oh, yes, massa, they fight like the devil!"
    Then pull off your coat and roll up your sleeve,
    For Richmond is a hard road to travel;
    Then pull off your coat and roll up your sleeve,
    For Richmond is a hard road to travel, I believe!

*The Battle of Cedar Rapids

East Virginia

A simple love song can be as significant a historical document as any other song describing a military or political event.

Virginia

I was born _____ in East Vir - gin - ia, _____ North Ca - ro - li _____ na I did go; _____ There I met _____ a fair young maid - en, _____ And whose name _____ I did not ___ know. _____

Well, her hair was dark of color,
Cheeks they were a rosy red.
On her breast she wore white lilies,
Where I longed to lay my head.

I'd rather live in some dark holler
Where the sun would never shine,
Than for you to love another,
And to know you'd never be mine.

I don't want your greenback dollar,
I don't want your silver chain;
All I want is your love darling,
Say that you'll be mine again.

A Native of Virginia. Courtesy of N.Y. Public Library Picture Collection.

John Hardy

STATE OF WEST VIRGINIA VS. JOHN HARDY. This day came again the State by her attorney and the prisoner who stands convicted of murder in the first degree was again brought to the bar of the Court in the custody of the sheriff of this County; and thereupon the prisoner being asked by the Court if anything he had or could say why the Court should not proceed to pass sentence of the law upon him...and the prisoner saying nothing...it is therefore considered by the Court that the prisoner John Hardy is guilty as found by the verdict of the jury herein and that the said John Hardy be hanged by the neck until he is dead...on Friday, the 19th day of January, 1894....

West Virginia

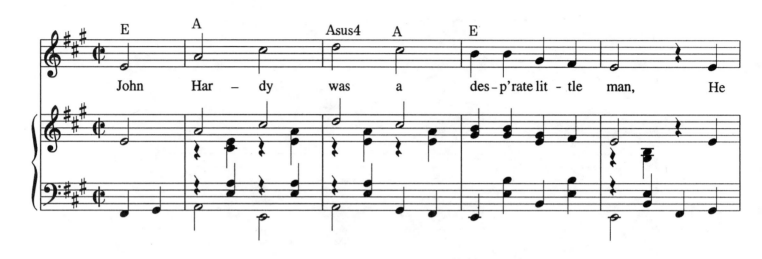

John Har – dy was a des – p'rate lit – tle man, He

wore two guns ev – 'ry day. _____ He

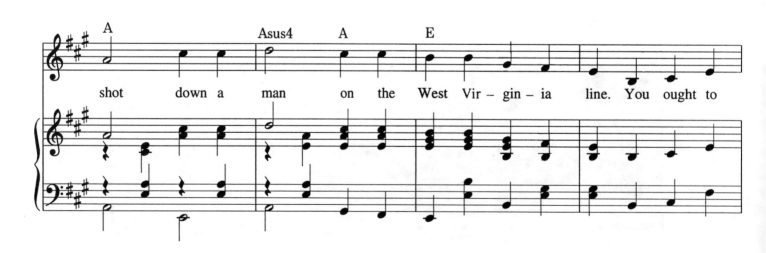

shot down a man on the West Vir – gin – ia line. You ought to

seen John ___ Har – dy get–tin' a – way, poor ___ boy, you ought to

seen John ___ Har – dy get–tin' a – way. ___

John Hardy stood at the gambling table.
Didn't have no interest in the game.
Up stepped a yellow gal and threw a dollar down,
Said, "John Hardy's playing in my name". (2)

John Hardy took that yellow gal's money,
And then he began to play.
Said, "The man that wins my yellow gal's dollar,
I'll lay him in his lonesome grave" (2)

John Hardy drew to a four-card straight,
And the cowboy drew to a pair.
John failed to catch and the cowboy won,
And he left him sitting dead in his chair. (2)

John started to catch that east-bound train,
So dark he could not see.
Up stepped the police and took him by the arm,
Said, "Johnny, come and go with me". (2)

John Hardy's father came to see him,
Come for to go his bail.
No bail was allowed for a murdering man,
So they shoved John Hardy back in Jail. (2)

They took John Hardy to the hanging ground,
And hung him there to die,
And the very last words I heard him say
Were, "My forty-four never told a lie". (2)

"I've been to the east and I've been to the west,
I've travelled this whole world around.
I've been to the river and I've been baptized,
And now I'm on my hanging ground". (2)

John Henry

"The Big Bend Tunnel on the C. and O. Road" cut through the rugged mountains along the New River. John Henry worked and died driving steel in the tunnel sometime around 1873. The ballad of John Henry describes him as larger than life, and indeed, his perhaps mythical race against the steam drill has been transformed into an allegorical epic of profound significance: man against the machine.

West Virginia

Well, __ ev – 'ry Mon – day __ morn-ing, _____ When the blue-birds be – gin to sing, _____ You can see John Hen – ry __ out __ on the line. __ You can hear __ John __ Hen – ry's ham – mer ring, __ Lord, __ Lord, __ You can hear __ John __

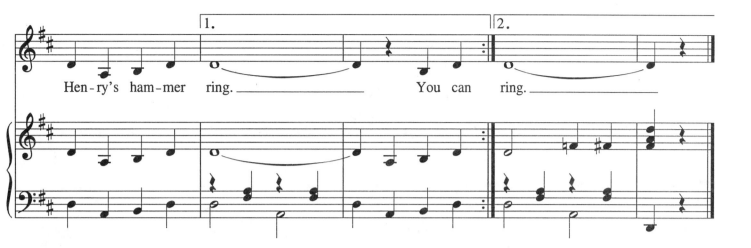

Hen - ry's ham - mer ring. _____ You can ring. _____

When John Henry was a little baby,
Sitting on his papa's knee,
Said, "That Big Bend Tunnel on the C and O Road,
It's gonna be the death of me." (2)

Well, the captain said to John Henry,
"Gonna bring me a steam drill 'round,
Gonna bring me a steam drill out on the job,
Gonna whup that steel on down." (2)

John Henry said to his captain,
"A man ain't nothin' but a man,
And before I let that steam drill beat me down,
I'll die with a hammer in my hand." (2)

John Henry said to his shaker,
"Shaker, why don't you pray?
'Cause if I miss this little piece of steel,
Tomorrow be your buryin' day." (2)

John Henry was driving on the mountain
And his hammer was flashing fire.
And the last words I heard that poor boy say,
"Gimme a cool drink of water 'fore I die." (2)

John Henry, he drove fifteen feet,
The steam drill only made nine.
But he hammered so hard that he broke his poor heart,
And he laid down his hammer and he died. (2)

They took John Henry to the graveyard
And they buried him in the sand.
And every locomotive comes a-roaring by says,
"There lies a steel-driving man." (2)

Freeze Fork on Scott's Run, West Virginia. Courtesy of N.Y. Public Library Picture Collection.

Southeast

Southeast

The March from Selma to Montgomery, Alabama, 1965. Courtesy of N.Y. Public Library Picture Collection.

Winnsboro Cotton Mill Blues

The Southern textile workers have produced a strikingly rich literature of songs of protest. Thousands of workers lured down from the Carolina hills to the mill towns by the promise of "good wages" in the 1920s were quickly treated to a rude and often brutal awakening. Seventy-hour work weeks were not uncommon — with an average take-home pay of $11 for men (and about half of that for some women). Attempts at unionization were met with violence and bloodshed (see "Chief Aderholt"). This sardonic song was based on the melody of a popular song of the day, "The Alcoholic Blues."

South Carolina

81

Chorus

Es – ki – mo pie. __ I got the blues, I got the blues, I got the

Winns – b'ro Cot – ton Mill blues. __ Lord – y, Lord – y,

spool – in's hard. __ You know and I know, I don't have to tell, You

work for Tom Wat – son, got to work like hell. I got the blues, I got the

82

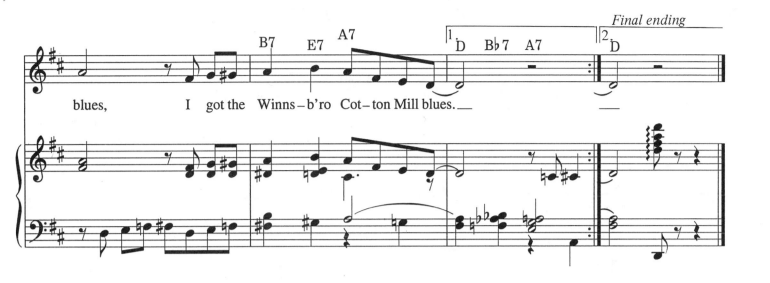

blues,   I got the Winns–b'ro Cot–ton Mill blues.___

When I die, don't bury me at all,
Just hang me up on the spool room wall.
Place a knotter in my right hand,
So I can keep on spoolin' in the promised land. *Chorus*

When I die, don't bury me deep,
Bury me down on 600 Street.
Place a bobbin in each hand,
So I can doff in the promised land. *Chorus*

Courtesy of N.Y. Public Library Picture Collection.

The Fall of Charleston

General Sherman, swinging northward from Savannah, Georgia, after "marching through Georgia," hoped to link up with General Grant, who would be coming down from the north. On February 18, 1865, after having overrun Columbia the day before, Sherman marched his army into Charleston. The war had gone full cycle, for it was upon Fort Sumter that the first Confederate shots of the Civil War had been fired almost four years earlier.

Words by Eugene T. Johnson
Music: "Whack Row De Dow"

South Carolina

Oh have you heard the glo—rious news, Is the cry from ev—'ry mouth,

Charles—ton is tak—en and the Reb—els put to rout; And

Beau—re—gard the chiv—al—rous, he ran to save his ba—con,__ When

he saw Gen—'ral Sher—man's Yanks, and "Charles—ton is tak—en!" With a

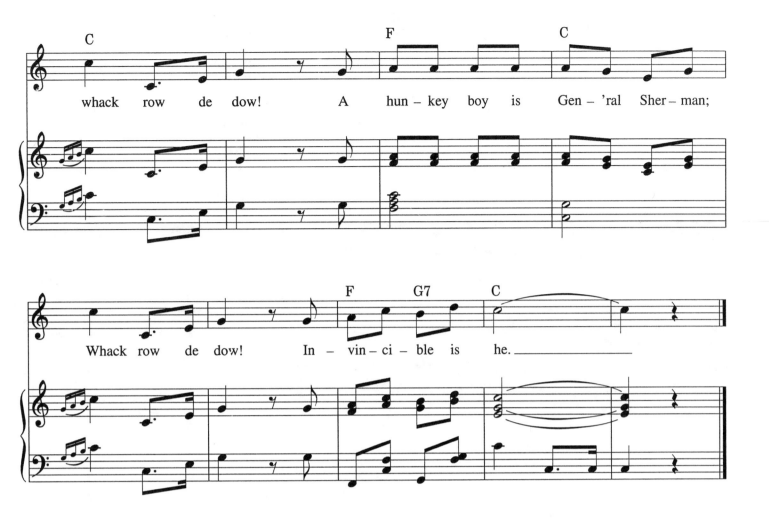

whack row de dow! A hun – key boy is Gen – 'ral Sher – man;

Whack row de dow! In – vin – ci – ble is he._____

The South Carolina chivalry,
They once did loudly boast;
That the footsteps of a Union man
Should ne'er pollute their coast.
They'd fight the Yankees two to one,
Who only fought for booty;
But when the "mudsills" came along,
It was "Legs do your duty!"
  With a whack row de dow!
  Babylon is fallen;
  Whack row de dow,
  The end is drawing near.

And from the "Sacred City,"
This valiant warlike throng
Skedaddled in confusion,
Although thirty thousand strong
Without a shot, without a blow,
Or least sign of resistance,
And leaving their poor friends behind,
With the "Yankees" for assistance.
  With a whack row de dow!
  How are you Southern chivalry?
  Whack row de dow!
  Your race is nearly run.

And again o'er Sumter's battered walls,
The Stars and Stripes do fly,
While the Chivalry of Sixty-one
In the "last ditch" lie;
With Sherman, Grant, and Porter, too,
To lead our men to glory;
We'll squash poor Jeff's Confederacy,
And then get "Hunkydory."
  With a whack row de dow!
  How are you neutral Johnny Bull?
  Whack row de dow!
  We'll settle next with you.

Mobile Bay

As a result of a charter dated December 17, 1819, granted by the first State Legislature of Alabama, Mobile became the commercial emporium for Alabama and Mississippi, its cotton exports increasing from 7,000 bales in 1818 to 100,000 in 1830 and 450,000 in 1840. The Mobile & Ohio Railroad, begun in 1848, provided ampler communication with the Mississippi valley, and Mobile's export of cotton rose to 1,000,000 bales in 1861. All this cotton was loaded onto ships on the backs of Negro stevedores, and it is from them that we get this song — a variant of a sailor's capstan shanty.

Alabama

Was you ev-er down in Mo-bile Bay? John-ny come tell us and

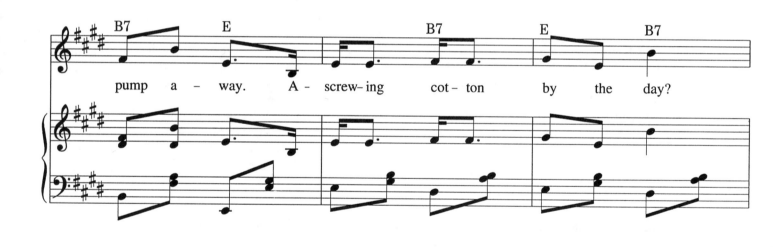

pump a-way. A-screw-ing cot-ton by the day?

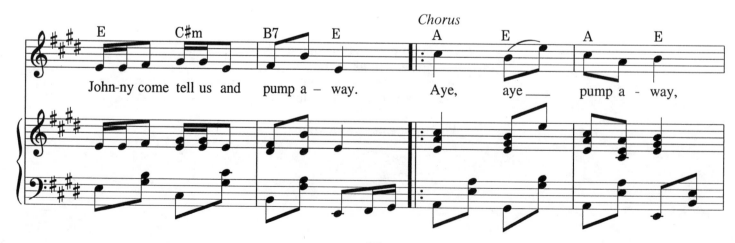

John-ny come tell us and pump a-way. *Chorus* Aye, aye___ pump a-way,

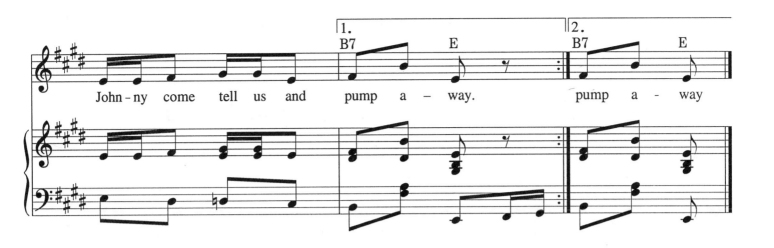

And how many bales can you carry on?
  Johnny come and tell us and pump away.
Just hurry up before she's gone.
  Johnny come and tell us and pump away. *Chorus*

The times are hard and the wages low,
  Johnny come and tell us and pump away.
Just one more bale before we go,
  Johnny come and tell us and pump away. *Chorus*

If ever good luck does come my way,
  Johnny come and tell us and pump away.
I'll say goodbye to Mobile Bay,
  Johnny come and tell us and pump away. *Chorus*

Mobile, Alabama, 1842. Courtesy of N.Y. Public Library Picture Collection.

Freedom's Coming and It Won't Be Long

On Mother's Day in 1961, a Trailways bus carrying a group of "Freedom Riders" pulled into the depot in Birmingham. The Freedom Riders were young people — black and white — who were challenging segregated seating on buses and segregation in general in southern cities. A mob was waiting as the bus arrived. No police were on the scene. The mob attacked the bus and its passengers. A similar violent incident had taken place a few weeks before in Anniston. In incidents like these, often when the police finally did arrive, it was to arrest the Freedom Riders, not the rioters.

Alabama

We took a trip on a Greyhound bus...
To fight segregation, this we must...

Violence in 'bama didn't stop our cause...
Federal marshals come enforce the laws...

On to Mississippi with speed we go...
Blue-shirted policemen meet us at the door...

Judge say local custom shall prevail...
We say "no" and we land in jail...

We're Coming, Arkansas

They say that a proposal was once introduced in the State Legislature to change the name of Arkansas. Whether this actually happened has always been a subject of speculation. Nevertheless, "speeches" purported to have been made in response to the proposal are part of Arkansas folklore:

Mr. Speaker, you blue-bellied rascal! I have for the last 30 minutes been trying to get your attention, and each time I have caught your eye, you have wormed, twisted and squirmed like a dog with a flea in his hide, damn you!

Gentlemen, you may tear down the honored pictures from the halls of the United States Senate, desecrate the grave of George Washington, haul down the Stars and Stripes, curse the Goddess of Liberty, and knock down the tomb of U.S. Grant, but your crime would in no wise compare in enormity with what you propose to do when you would change the name of Arkansas! Change the name of Arkansas — hell-fire, no!

Compare the lily of the valley to the gorgeous sunrise; the discordant croak of the bullfrog to the melodious tones of a nightingale; the classic strains of Mozart to the bray of a Mexican mule; the puny arm of a Peruvian prince to the muscles of a Roman gladiator — but never change the name of Arkansas. Hell, no!

Arkansas

90

four - horse team will soon be seen on the road to Ar - kan - sas.

The men keep hounds down there,
And hunting is all they care;
The women plough and hoe the corn,
While the men shoot turkey and deer.   *Chorus*

The girls are strong down there,
Clean and healthy and gay,
They card and spin from morning till night
And dance from night till day.   *Chorus*

They raise their 'baccer patch,
The women all smoke and chaw,
Eat hog, and hominy and poke for greens
Way down in Arkansas.   *Chorus*

The roads are rough down there,
You must take um 'done or raw'
There's rocks and rills and stumps and hills
On the road to Arkansas.   *Chorus*

A "Blaze" of '38 and The Arkansas Traveller.
Courtesy of N.Y. Public Library Picture Collection.

Marching Song of the First Arkansas Regiment

This is the marching song of the First Arkansas Negro Regiment. It was not until the Civil War was quite advanced that widespread recruiting of Negroes into the Union Army was undertaken. White officers commanded these outfits, and Captain Lindley Miller, a white officer of the "First Arkansas," is credited with writing the words to this song. The song caught on and was published by the Supervisory Committee for Recruiting Colored Regiments.

Arkansas

Oh, we're the bul – ly sol – diers of the "First of Ar – kan-sas," We are fight – ing for the un – ion, we are fight – ing for the law. We can hit a Reb– el fur– ther than a white man ev – er saw, As we go march-ing on

Chorus

Glo – ry, gol–ry, hal – le – lu – jah, Glo – ry, glo–ry, hal – le – lu – jah,

Glo – ry, glo – ry, hal – le – lu – jah, As we go march–ing on.

See, there above the center, where the flag is waving bright,
We are going out of slavery; we're bound for freedom's light;
We mean to show Jeff Davis how the Africans fight,
As we go marching on!   *Chorus*

We have done with hoeing cotton, we have done with hoeing corn,
We are colored Yankee soldiers, now, as sure as you are born;
When the masters hear us yelling, they'll think it's Gabriel's horn,
As we go marching on.   *Chorus*

They will have to pay us wages, the wages of their sin,
They will have to bow their foreheads to their colored kith and kin,
They will have to give us house-room, or the roof shall tumble in!
As we go marching on.   *Chorus*

We heard the Proclamation, master hush it as he will,
The bird he sing it to us, hoppin' on the cotton hill,
And the possum up the gum tree, he couldn't keep it still,
As he went climbing on.   *Chorus*

They said, "Now colored brethren, you shall be forever free,
From the first of January, Eighteen hundred sixty-three."
We heard it in the river going rushing to the sea,
As it went sounding on.   *Chorus*

Father Abraham has spoken and the message has been sent,
The prison doors he opened, and out the pris'ners went,
To join the sable army of the "African descent,"
As we go marching on.   *Chorus*

Then fall in, colored brethren, you'd better do it soon,
Don't you hear the drum a-beating the Yankee Doodle tune?
We are with you now this morning, we'll be far away at noon,
As we go marching on.   *Chorus*

Benjamin Beall in the Florida War

By the treaty of 1819, Spain formally ceded Florida to the United States. Indian affairs furnished the most serious problems of the new Territory of Florida. By treaties at Payne's Landing in 1832 and Fort Gibson in 1833, the Indian chiefs agreed to exchange their Florida lands for equal territory in the western part of the United States. But a strong sentiment against removal suddenly developed, and the efforts of the U.S. government to enforce the treaties brought on the Seminole War (1836–42), which resulted in the forcible removal of all but a few hundred Seminoles.

Florida

Words by Colonel A. T. Lee
Music by Jerry Silverman

Oh, a jol-ly brave knight was our Ben-ja-min Beall, In the Flo-ri-da War;_____ As man-y a jol-ly bright camp-fire could tell In the Flo-ri-da war._____ Oh! the sto-ries he told that nev-er grow old, And the songs that he trolled un-til

re - veil - le rolled, Made ___ chiefs and sub - al - terns as mer - ry as bold, In the

1.2. Flo - ri - da war, ___

3. *Final ending* Who was toil and cold lead In the Flo - ri - da war. ___

Who was brave as a lion, yet soft as a child
        In the Florida War?
Who could swim the Suwanee when waters were wild
        In the Florida War?
Who could harass Sam Jones till he ached in his bones,
Rap a redskin whilst laughing, then weep o'er his groans
Then chant him a requiem in reverent tones,
        In the Florida War?

Who, when shattered and broken, from scoutings and toils,
        In the Florida War,
Could smile at grim death as he felt its cold coils,
        In the Florida War?
Who but valiant old Ben - beau ideal of men,
Who wore gay soldier's togs in the days that we ken,
God rest his old head where his blanket is spread
Far from toil and cold lead,
        In the Florida War.

The West Palm Beach Hurricane

Another view of the south Florida hurricane of September 16, 1928, takes a somewhat uncharitable view of its victims:

God A'mighty moved on the water,
And the people in Miami run.
Ships swam down that ocean,
It was most too sad to tell;
Ten thousand people got drownded,
And all went to Hell but twelve.

(Excerpt from "Miami Hairikin")

Florida

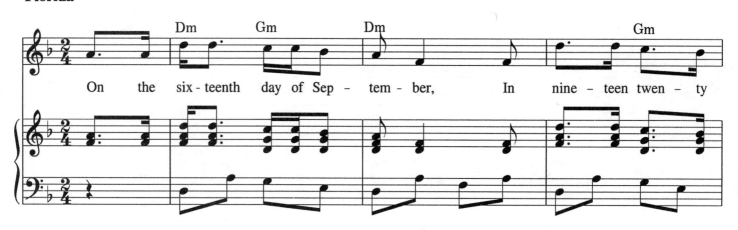

On the six-teenth day of Sep - tem - ber, In nine - teen twen - ty

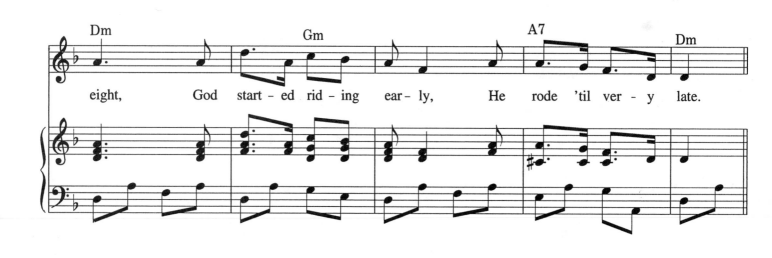

eight, God start - ed rid - ing ear - ly, He rode 'til ver - y late.

In the storm, Oh in the storm, ___ Lord, some

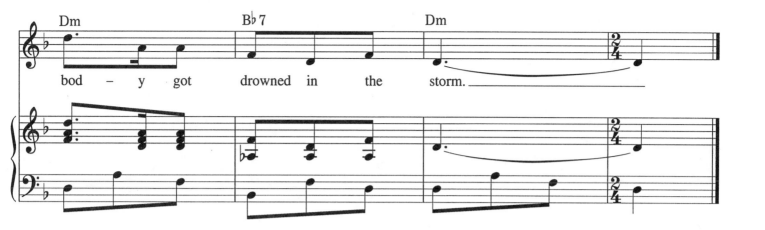

bod — y got drowned in the storm. _____

He rode out on the ocean,
Chained the lightning to his wheel,
Stepped on land at West Palm Beach,
And the wicked hearts did yield.   *Chorus*

Over in Pahokee,
Families rushed out at the door,
And somebody's poor mother
Haven't been seen anymore.   *Chorus*

Some mothers looked at their children,
As they began to cry,
Cried, "Lord, have mercy,
For we all must die."   *Chorus*

I tell you wicked people,
What you had better do;
Go down and get the Holy Ghost
And then you live the life, too.   *Chorus*

Out around Okeechobee,
All scattered on the ground,
The last account of the dead they had
Were twenty-two hundred found.   *Chorus*

South Bay, Belleglade, and Pahokee,
Tell me they all went down,
And over at Chosen,
Everybody got drowned.   *Chorus*

Some people are yet missing,
And haven't been found, they say.
But this we know, they will come forth
On the Resurrection Day.   *Chorus*

When Gabriel sounds the trumpet,
And the dead begin to rise,
I'll meet the saints from Chosen,
Up in the heavenly skies.   *Chorus*

Courtesy of N.Y. Public Library Picture Collection.

Goober Peas

Goober peas are peanuts, which constituted an ever-increasing proportion of many Confederate soldiers' diets in the waning days of the Civil War. This song first appeared in print after the war, in 1866, with words credited to "A. Pindar, Esq." and music to "P. Nutt, Esq." — both, of course, being *noms de goober*.

Georgia

When a horseman passes, the soldiers have a rule,
To cry out at their loudest, "Mister, here's your mule!"
But another pleasure enchantinger than these,
Is wearing out your grinders, eating goober peas! *Chorus*

Just before the battle the Gen'ral hears a row,
He says, "The Yanks are coming, I hear their rifles now."
He turns around in wonder, and what do you think he sees?
The Georgia Militia - eating goober peas! *Chorus*

I think my song has lasted almost long enough,
The subject's interesting, but rhymes are mighty rough,
I wish this war was over, when free from rags and fleas,
We'd kiss our wives and sweethearts and gobble goober peas! *Chorus*

Marching Through Georgia

On December 21, 1864, Abraham Lincoln received the following telegram from General William Tecumseh Sherman:

I beg to present you as a Christmas gift, the city of Savannah, with one hundred and fifty guns and plenty of ammunition, and also about 25,000 bales of cotton.

Sherman's "Lost Army" had been on the march through Georgia "from Atlanta to the sea" since November 15. For six weeks all telegraphic communication from the army had been severed — until that memorable telegram arrived at the White House. The Confederacy had been effectively split in two. The war would soon be over.

Georgia

Words and Music by Henry C. Work

Bring the good old bu – gle, boys, we'll sing an – oth – er song; Sing it with a spir – it that will start the world a – long, Sing it as we used to sing it,

fif-ty thou-sand strong, While we were march-ing through Geor - gia. Hur-

rah! Hur-rah! We bring the ju - bi - lee! Hur - rah! Hur rah! The

flag that makes you free! So we sang the cho-rus from At -

lan-ta to the sea, While we were march - ing through Geor - gia.

How the black folks shouted when they heard the joyful sound!
How the turkeys gobbled which our commissary found!
How the sweet potatoes even started from the ground,
  While we were marching through Georgia.   *Chorus*

Yes, and there were Union men who wept with joyful tears,
When they saw the honored flag they had not seen for years;
Hardly could they be restrained from breaking forth in cheers,
  While we were marching through Georgia.   *Chorus*

"Sherman's dashing Yankee boys will never reach the coast!"
So the saucy Rebels said, and 'twas a handsome boast;
Had they not forgot, alas! to reckon with the host,
  While we were marching through Georgia.   *Chorus*

So we made a throughfare for Freedom and her train,
Sixty miles in latitude, three hundred to the main;
Treason fled before us, for resistance was in vain,
  While we were marching through Georgia.   *Chorus*

Atlanta, Georgia. Courtesy of N.Y. Public Library Picture Collection.

The Battle of New Orleans

The Treaty of Ghent, ending hostilities between England and the United States in the War of 1812, was signed on December 24, 1814. The Battle of New Orleans, in which American forces under Andrew Jackson defeated the British under Sir Edward Pakenham, was fought some two weeks later, on January 8, 1815. Communications being what they were, neither army was aware of the treaty at the time of the battle.

Louisiana

'Twas on the eighth of __ Jan - u - a - ry, just at the dawn of day, We
spied those Brit - ish __ of - fi - cers All __ dressed in bat'l ar - ray. Old
Jack - son then gave __ or - ders: Each man to keep his post, And
form a line from __ right to left, And __ let no time be lost.

With rockets and with bombshells, like comets we let fly;
Like lions they advanced us, the fate of war to try;
Large streams of fiery vengeance upon them we let pour,
While many a brave commander lay withering in his gore.

Thrice they marched up to charge, and thrice they gave the ground;
We fought them full three hours, then bugle horns did sound.
Great heaps of human pyramids lay strewn before our eyes;
We blew the horns and rang the bells to drown their dying cries.

Come all you British noblemen and listen unto me;
Our Frontiersman has proved to you America is free.
But tell your royal master when you return back home,
That out of thirty thousand men, but few of you returned.

Death of Pakenham at the Battle of New Orleans. Courtesy of N.Y. Public Library Picture Collection.

House of the Rising Sun

Basin Street—a product of Victorian hypocrisies, of the double standard of morality—gave employment to some marvelous and unique musicians like Jelly Roll Morton, Buddy Bolden, King Oliver, and Louis Armstrong. There were houses like Lulu's Mahogany Hall, where string trios and small jazz combinations produced one of the most vital and creative periods of the art.... But the misery-breeding side of life was there, and perhaps it is best that it not be forgotten in the re-telling of old legends. This was in the days before...a great German doctor's discovery of a way to administer silver solution to human body to kill the syphilis germ.... It was a day when victims of the shadow-plague walked the streets of New Orleans...living corpses, eyelids dropping in early paralysis, hands and body shaking with a palsy not caused by old age. (Thomas Sancton, writing in the *New Orleans Item* in 1950, when Lulu's Mahogany Hall was finally torn down)

Louisiana

There is a __ house in __ New Or - leans they call the Ris - ing __ Sun. _____ It has been the ru - in of ma-ny a poor __ girl, and me, oh, Lord, __ was __ one. _____ If __

If I had listened what Mama said,
I'd a' been at home today,
Being so young and foolish,
Poor girl, let a gambler lead me astray.

My mother, she's a tailor,
She sold those new blue jeans;
My sweetheart, he's a drunkard, Lord,
Drinks down in New Orleans.

The only thing a drunkard needs
Is a suitcase and a trunk
The only time he's satisfied
Is when he's on a drunk.

Go tell my baby sister,
Never do like I have done,
To shun that house in New Orleans
They call the Rising Sun.

One foot is on the platform
And the other one on the train,
I'm going back to New Orleans
To wear that ball and chain.

I'm going back to New Orleans,
My race is almost run,
Going back to spend the rest of my life
Beneath that Rising Sun.

Marketing in New Orleans. Courtesy of N.Y. Public Library Picture Collection.

Vicksburg Blues

The blues are one of the great contributions made by the Negro people to American culture. Further, the blues are one of the significant — perhaps *the* significant — contributions of American music to world culture. Taken as a whole, the blues are an expression of a way of life; or rather, individual reactions to a way of life — variations on a theme. The cotton fields, the levees, and the prisons of Mississippi have been among the most fertile areas for black blues singers — singers whose stark lives are mirrored in those unique three-line verses that we call "the blues."

Mississippi

I've got those Vicks-burg blues and I'm ___ sing-in' it ev-'ry-where I go. ___

I've got those Vicks-burg blues and I'm ___

sing-in' it ev-'ry-where I go. ___ Now, the

108

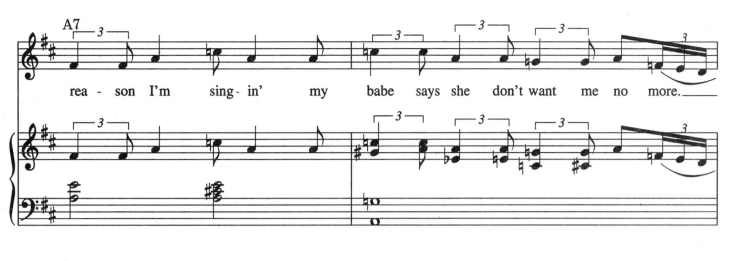

rea - son I'm sing - in' my babe says she don't want me no more.

1.
D   A7

Final ending
D   G7   D

I've got those

I've got those Vicksburg blues and I'm singin'
   it everywhere I please.
I've got those Vicksburg blues and I'm singin'
   it everywhere I please.
Now, the reason I'm singin' it is to give my poor
   heart some ease.

Now, I don't like this place, mama, and I never
   will.
Now, I don't like this place, mama, and I never
   will.
I can sit right there in jail and look at Vicksburg
   on the hill.

Vicksburg, Mississippi. Courtesy of N.Y. Public Library Picture Collection.

Casey Jones

John Luther Jones (called Casey for his hometown of Cayce, Kentucky) pulled engine Number 638 hauling the Cannonball Express on the Illinois Central Line out of Memphis, Tennessee, at 11:00 at night on April 29, 1906. He was heading south for Canton, Mississippi, in a light rain. Down the track, ahead of Casey at Vaughn, Mississippi, a long freight train was being switched off the main line onto a siding. The Cannonball was doing 60 m.p.h. into Vaughn when Casey saw the last of the boxcars 100 feet ahead. With no time to stop, he shouted to his fireman, Sim Webb, to jump. When the wreck was untangled, Casey was found with one hand on the brakes and the other on the whistle cord.

Mississippi

Come all you roun-ders that ____ want ____ to hear, The
cal - ler called Cas - ey at ____ half ____ past four, He

sto - ry of ____ a ____ brave en - gi - neer.
kissed his wife ____ at the sta - tion door, He

Cas - ey Jones ____ was the round - er's name, On a
mount - ed to the cab - in with his or - ders in his hand, And he

Well Casey Jones was all right.
He stuck to his duty day and night.
They loved his whistle and his ring number three,
And he came into Memphis on the old I. C.
Out of South Memphis yard on the fly,
Heard the fireman say, "You got a white eye."
Well, the switchman knew by the engine moan
That the man at the throttle was Casey Jones. *Chorus*

The rain was comin' down five or six weeks.
The railroad track was like the bed of a creek.
They slowed her down to a thirty-mile gait
And the south-bound mail was eight hours late.
Fireman says, "Casey, you're runnin' too fast,
You run that block board the last station you passed."
Casey says, "I believe we'll make it though,
For she steams a lot better than I ever know." *Chorus*

Casey says, "Fireman, don't you fret,
Keep knockin' at the fire door, don't give up yet,
I'm going to run her till she leaves the rail,
Or make it on time with the south-bound mail."
Around the curve and down the dump,
Two locomotives was a bound to jump,
Fireman hollered, "Casey, it's just ahead,
We might jump and make it but we'll all be dead." *Chorus*

The locomotives met in the middle of the hill,
In a head-on tangle that's bound to kill,
He tried to do his duty, the yard men said,
But Casey Jones was scalded dead.
Headaches and heartaches and all kinds of pain
They all ride along with the railroad train,
Stories of brave men, noble and grand,
Belong to the life of the railroad man. *Chorus*

Courtesy of N.Y. Public Library Picture Collection.

Great Lakes

Great Lakes

Detroit, Michigan. Courtesy of N.Y. Public Library Picture Collection.

El-A-Noy

Among the pioneers were boomers, boosters. About the time this song came, the Shawneetown Advocate, *only newspaper in seven counties of southern Illinois, was proclaiming its ideal to be "universal liberty abroad, and an ocean-bound republic at home." In northern Illinois, the* Gem of the Prairie, *a weekly magazine published in Chicago, was declaring, "The West must have a literature peculiarly its own. It is here that the great problem of human destiny will be worked out on a grander scale than was ever before attempted or conceived." (*The American Songbag *by Carl Sandburg, 1927)*

Illinois

Way down up-on the Wa-bash, Such land was nev-er known. If Ad-am had passed o-ver it, the soil he'd sure-ly own. He'd think it was the gar-den he'd played in when a boy, And straight pro-nounce it E-den in the State of El-a-noy. Then

move your fam – 'ly west – ward, Good health you will en – joy, And
rise to wealth and hon – or in the State of El – a – noy.

'Twas here the Queen of Sheba came,
With Solomon of old,
With an ass-load of spices,
Pomegranates and fine gold;
And when she saw this lovely land,
Her heart was filled with joy,
Straightway she said: "I'd like to be
A Queen in El-a-noy." *Chorus*

She's bounded by the Wabash,
The Ohio and the Lakes,
She's crawfish in the swampy lands,
The milk-sick and the shakes;
But these are slight diversions
And take not from the joy
Of living in this garden land,
The State of El-a-noy. *Chorus*

Away up in the northward,
Right on the border line,
A great commercial city,
Chicago, you will find.
Her men are all like Abelard,
Her women like Heloise;
All honest virtuous people,
For they live in El-a-noy. *Chorus*

Cairo

The southern Illinois riverport of Cairo was a key military objective in the Civil War battles along the Mississippi and the struggle for control of the West. Major General John C. Fremont, then in command of the "Western Department," embracing Illinois and all states west of the Mississippi, wrote after the war: "Among the various points threatened, Cairo was the key to the success of my operations. The waterways and the district around Cairo were of first importance. Upon the possession of this district depended the descent and control of the Mississippi Valley by the Union armies, or the inroad by the Confederate forces into the loyal states."

Illinois

There's a place out West where the Un-ion troops Take toll from the Reb-el ___ ships and sloops; And if down the riv-er a craft would go, She must rec-og-nize a cus-tom house at Ca-i-ro.

Chorus

Ca-i-ro, Oh, ___ Ca-i-ro! There's no giv-ing that the ___

116

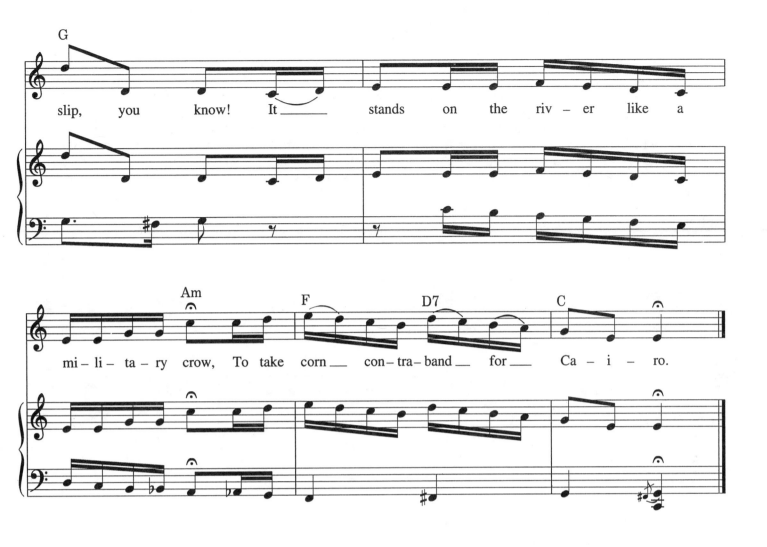

slip, you know! It ___ stands on the riv – er like a mi – li – ta – ry crow, To take corn ___ con – tra – band ___ for ___ Ca – i – ro.

The rolling Mississippi was a highway free,
When the people down in Dixie acted honestly;
But since like plunderers they've cut up so,
They'll have to pay a floating tax to Ca-i-ro!
 Ca-i-ro, Oh, Ca-i-ro!
 The Southrons say it's a precious go,
 That they can't send a boat for a bit of tow,
 But it has to take an overhaul at Ca-i-ro.

The Southern chivaligators now, they say,
To capture the place are on their way;
But if they'd take *my* advice they'd never try to go
Within telescopic range of Ca-i-ro!
 Ca-i-ro, Oh, Ca-i-ro!
 The Union guns are mounted so,
 That if once sighted at a nearby foe,
 They'd make a perfect graveyard of Ca-i-ro.

Bold Prentiss holds the chief command,
And prime Jim Lane is close at hand;
They are bound by their honors to do nothing slow,
But to take a river revenue at Ca-i-ro!
 Ca-i-ro, Oh, Ca-i-ro!
 There's no giving that the slip, you know;
 And if down the river the traitors want to go,
 They'll have to get their baggage *checked* at Ca-i-ro!

Tip and Ty

The presidential election campaign of 1840, which pitted William Henry Harrison against Martin Van Buren, was the first great singing campaign. Harrison had been governor of Indiana in 1809 when he entered into a series of negotiations with the great Indian leader Tecumseh over the question of Indian territory and "cessions" to white settlers west of the Ohio. The British encouraged the Indians to resist these cessions. As a result, military action against the Indians was undertaken, and Harrison led a victory over the Indians at the Tippecanoe River (near the present Lafayette, Indiana) on November 7, 1811. This victory established Harrison's military reputation. By the time the 1840 election rolled around, he was known as "Old Tippecanoe" or simply "Tip." Harrison won the election, but died after only one month in office (April 4, 1841). He was succeeded by "Ty," his vice president, John Tyler.

Indiana

What's the cause of this com-mo-tion, mo-tion, mo-tion, Our coun-try through? It

is the ball that's roll – ing on, For Tip-pe-can-oe and Ty – ler too, For

Tip-pe-can-oe and Ty – ler too, And with them __ we'll beat lit – tle Van, Van,

Van;   Van is a   used – up man. And with them ___ we'll beat lit – tle   Van.

Like the rushing of mighty waters, waters, waters,
On it will go!
And in its course will clear the way
For Tippecanoe and Tyler too. *Chorus*

See the Loco standard tottering, tottering, tottering,
Down it must go!
And in its place we'll rear the flag
Of Tippecanoe and Tyler too. *Chorus*

The Bay State boys turned out in thousands, thousands,
Not long ago,   /thousands,
And at Bunker Hill they set their seals
For Tippecanoe and Tyler too. *Chorus*

Have you heard from old Vermount, mount, mount,
All honest and true?
The Green Mountain boys are rolling the ball
For Tippecanoe and Tyler too. *Chorus*

Don't you hear from every quarter, quarter, quarter,
Good news and true?
That swift the ball is rolling on
For Tippecanoe and Tyler too. *Chorus*

Now you hear the Vanjacks talking, talking, talking,
Things look quite blue,
For all the world seems turning round
For Tippecanoe and Tyler too. *Chorus*

Let them talk about hard cider, cider, cider,
And Log Cabins too,
It will only help to speed the ball
For Tippecanoe and Tyler too. *Chorus*

His latchstring hangs outside the door, door, door,
And is never pulled through,
For it never was the custom of
Old Tippecanoe and Tyler too. *Chorus*

He always has his tables set, set, set,
For all honest and true,
To ask you in to take a bite
With Tippecanoe and Tyler too. *Chorus*

See the spoilsmen and leg-treasurers, treasurers, treasurers,
All in a stew!
For well they know they stand no chance
With Tippecanoe and Tyler too. *Chorus*

Little Matty's days are numbered, **numbered,** numbered,
Out he must go!
And in his place we'll put the good
Old Tippecanoe and Tyler too. *Chorus*

On the Banks of the Wabash, Far Away

Paul Dresser was born in Terre Haute, on the banks of the Wabash. This, his most famous song, was written in 1899. Within a year it had sold a million copies of sheet music. Its sentimental character is right in line with the way Americans viewed themselves and "the good old days" around the turn of the century. In 1913 it became the official state song of Indiana.

Indiana

By Paul Dresser

first re–ceived my les–sons, na–ture's school.　　　　　　　But
There I begged of her to be my bride.　　　　　　　Long

one thing there is mis–sing in the pic–ture,　　　　　　With –
years have passed since I strolled thro' the church – yard,　　　She's

out her face it seems so in–com–plete.　　　　　I
sleep–ing there, my an–gel Ma–ry dear.　　　　　I

long to see my moth–er in the door – way,　　　　As she
loved her, but she thought I did – n't mean it.　　　　Still I'd

122

Michigania

It was exceptional for a settler to emigrate directly from his place of birth to Michigan. He was much more likely to have a number of intermediary stopping places; for example, he might be born in England, migrate with his parents to Connecticut, be educated in Vermont, engage in business in New York, and then spend some years on the frontier in Ohio, and perhaps return to New York before finally settling in Michigan. (Economic and Social Beginnings of Michigan by George Newman Fuller, 1916)

Michigan

For there's your Penobscot way down in parts of Maine,
Where timber grows in plenty but not a bit of grain,
And there is your Quaddy and your Piscataqua,
But these can't hold a candle to Michigania.

And there's the state of Vermont, but what a place is that?
To be sure the girls are pretty and the cattle very fat.
But who among her mountains and clouds of snow would stay,
While he can buy a section in Michigania?

And there is Massachusetts, once good enough, be sure,
But now she is always lying in taxation and manure.
She'll cause a peck of trouble but deal a peck will pay,
While all is scripture measure in Michigania.

And there's the land of Blue Laws where deacons cut their hair,
For fear their locks and tenons will not exactly square.
Where beer that works on Sunday a penalty must pay,
While all is free and easy in Michigania.

And there's the state of New York, the people's very rich;
Among themselves and others have dug a mighty ditch
Which renders it more easy for us to find the way,
And sail upon the waters of Michigania.

What country ever grew up so great in little time,
Just popping from a nursery right into life its prime?
When Uncle Sam did wean her, 'twas but the other day,
And now she's quite a lady, this Michigania.

And if you want to go to a place called Washtenaw,
You'll first upon the Huron; such land you never saw,
Where ships come to Ann Arbor right through a pleasant bay,
And touch at Ypsilanti in Michigania.

And if you want to go a little farther back,
You'll find the shire of Oakland, the town of Pontiac,
Which springing up so sudden scared the wolves and bears away,
That used to roam about there in Michigania.

And if you want to go where Rochester is there,
And farther still Mt. Clemens looks out upon St. Clair.
Besides some other places within McCombia,
That promise population to Michigania.

And if you want to travel a little farther on,
I guess you'll touch St. Joseph where everybody's gone,
Where everything like Jack's bean grows monstrous fast, they say,
And beats the rest all hollow in Michigania.

Come, all ye Yankee farmer boys with metal hearts like me,
And elbow grease in plenty to bow the forest tree,
Come, buy a quarter section, and I'll be bound you'll say,
This country takes the rag off, this Michigania.

Detroit Skating Rink. Courtesy of N.Y. Public Library Picture Collection.

Michigan Water Blues

The lure of the industrial North was a powerful magnet for many thousands of poor Southern blacks. They saw it as an opportunity to break the cycle of sharecropping and menial labor, always hemmed in by Jim Crow laws and social customs. The automobile assembly lines of Detroit were the goal of many of these people.

Michigan

126

I

I believe to my soul I've got to leave this place,
Goin' away where the folks don't know my face.
Michigan water tastes like sherry wine.

II

Gal in Lou'siana - one in Maine,
Got one in Mississippi, scared to call her name.
Michigan water tastes like sherry wine,
Michigan water tastes like sherry wine.

The Death of Colonel Crafford

Colonel Crawford ("Crafford") led his men on a murderous raid against the Christian Delaware Indians in the Moravian villages on the banks of the Sandusky River on May 25, 1782. His troops met a disastrous defeat. All were eventually killed, including Crawford, who was burned at the stake on June 11. The renegade Simon Girty ("Girtee") witnessed the scene with great satisfaction.

Ohio

Music by Jerry Silverman

A bold-hearted company, as we do hear,
Equipped themselves, being all volunteers;
In number four hundred eighty-nine,
To take Sandusky town was their design.

In seventeen hundred eighty-two,
In May the twenty-sixth, as I tell unto you,
They crossed the Ohio, as we do understand,
Where brave Colonel Crafford he gave the command.

With spirits undaunted away they did steer
Through the Indian country without dread or fear,
Where Nicholas Slover and Jonathan Deans
Conducted them over the Sandusky plains.

Our brave Colonel Crafford and officer bold,
On the fourth of June did the Indians behold;
On the plains of Sandusky at three the same day,
Both armies approached in battle array.

The Indians on horseback, Girtee gave the command;
On the side of the plain they boldly did stand;
Our men, like brave heroes, upon them did fire,
Till backwards the Indians were forced to retire.

Our rifles did rattle, and bullets did fly,
Till some of our men on the ground they did lie,
And some being wounded, to others they said,
"Fight on, brother soldiers, and don't be dismayed."

Brave Colonel Williamson, as we do understand,
He prayed for three hundred men at his command;
And, had it been granted, we make no great doubt,
We'd put the vile savages all to the rout.

Like a hero of old there was brave Major Light
Who encouraged his men for to stand and to fight;
And with courage and conduct his men did command,
Like a Grecian that hero in battle did stand.

There was brave Major Briston, the fourth in command,
In the front of the battle most boldly did stand,
And with heroic courage his post did maintain,
While bullets like hail in great showers did rain.

There was brave Bibbs and Ogle received a ball;
On the plains of Sandusky they nobly did fall;
And not them alone, but some more of their train
Had the honor of death on the Sandusky plain.

Our officers all so most nobly did fight,
And likewise our men, from two days until night,
Till a reinforcement of Indians there came,
Which made us retreat from the Sandusky plain.

"Now," says our commander, "since we have lost ground,
And with greater numbers they do us surround,
We'll gather the wounded men, and let us save
All that's able to walk, and the rest we must leave."

Our brave Colonel Crafford, upon his retreat,
Likewise Major Harrison and Doctor Knight
With Slover, their pilot, and several men,
Were made prisoners of war on the Sandusky plain.

And now they have taken these men of renown,
And dragged them away to the Sandusky town;
In their cruel council condemned to be
Burnt alive at the stake by cruel Girtee.

They, like diabolians, this act did pursue,
And Girtee the head of the infernal crew;
This insidiator was a-standing by
While they in the fire bodies did fry.

The scalps of their heads while alive they did tear,
Their bodies with irons red hot they did sear;
They bravely expired without ever a groan
That might have melted a heart was harder than a stone.

And when our brave heroes was burnt at the stake,
Brave Knight and brave Slover they made their escape;
With kind heaven's assistance they brought us the news,
So none need the truth of these tidings refuse.

From east unto west, let it be understood;
Let everyone arise to revenge Crafford's blood,
And likewise the blood of those men of renown,
That was taken and burnt at Sandusky town.

Perry's Victory

The most important naval battle of the War of 1812 was fought near Put-in-Bay in Lake Erie off the coast near Port Clinton. There, on September 10, 1813, an American fleet commanded by Commodore Oliver Hazard Perry met and defeated a British squadron of six ships under the command of Captain Robert H. Barclay. As a result of Perry's triumph, the British were forced to evacuate Detroit, ultimately guaranteeing that the United States would not be compelled to cede any territory to Britain at the cessation of hostilities. Perry is remembered for this victory and for the famous message that he sent to General William Henry Harrison ("Tippecanoe"): "We have met the enemy and they are ours; two ships, two brigs, one schooner, and one sloop."

Ohio

Ye tars of Co – lum – bia, give ear to my sto – ry, Who
val – or has gained you im – mor – tal glo – ry, A

fought with brave Per – ry where can – nons did roar; Your lum – bi – an
fame that shall last un – til time is no more. Co –

tars are the true sons of Mars. They rake for and aft as they

fight on the deep. On the bed of lake E – rie, com – mand – ed by

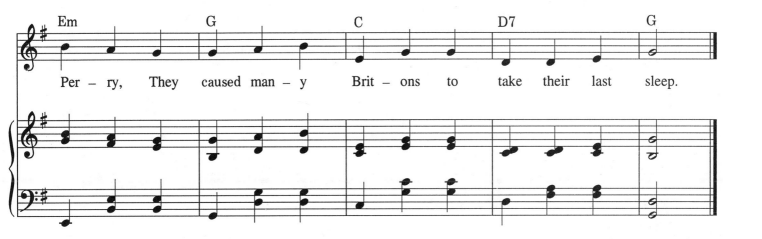

Per - ry,   They   caused man - y   Brit - ons   to   take   their   last   sleep.

'Twas just at sunrise, and a glorious day,
Our squadron at anchor, snug in Put-in-Bay;
When we saw the bold Britons and cleared for a bout,
Instead of Put-in, by the Lord, we put out.
Up went Union Jack, never up there before,
"Don't give up the ship!" was the motto it bore;
And as soon as that motto our gallant lads saw,
They thought of their Lawrence and shouted, "Huzza!"

O, then, 'twould have raised your hat three inches higher,
To see how we dashed in among them like fire;
The *Lawrence* went first, and the rest as they could,
And a long time the brunt of the battle she stood.
'Twas peppering work - fire, fury and smoke
And groans, that from wounded lads spite of them broke;
The water grew red round our ship as she lay,
Though 'twas never before so till that bloody day.

They fell all around me, like spars in a gale,
The shot made a sieve of each rag of a sail;
And out of our crew, scarce a dozen remained,
But these gallant tars still the battle maintained.
'Twas then our Commander - God bless his young heart! —
Thought it best from his well-peppered ship to depart,
And bring up the rest who were tugging behind,
For why? They were sadly in want of a wind.

Then to Yarnall he gave the command of the ship,
And set out like a lark on his desperate trip,
In a small open yawl, right through their whole fleet,
Who with many a broadside our cock-boat did greet.
I steered her and, damn me, if every inch
Of these timbers of mine at each crack didn't flinch;
But our tight little Commodore, cool and serene,
To still ne'er a muscle by any was seen.

Whole volleys of muskets were levelled at him,
But the devil a one ever grazed e'en a limb,
Though he stood up erect in the stern of the boat,
Till the crew pulled him down by the skirts of his coat.
At length, through Heaven's mercy, we reached the other ship,
And the wind springing up, we gave her the whip,
And ran down the line, boys, through thick and through thin,
And bothered their ears with a horrible din.

Then starboard and larboard, and this way and that,
We banged 'em and raked 'em and laid their masts flat;
Till one after t'other they hauled down their flag,
And an end put for that time to Johnny Bull's brag.
The *Detroit* and *Queen Charlotte* and *Lady Prevost*,
Not able to fight or run, gave up the ghost;
And not one of them all from our grapplings got free,
Though we'd just fifty-four guns and they'd sixty-three.

Now give us a bumper to Elliot and those
Who came up in good time to belabor our foes;
To our fresh-water sailors we'll toss off one more,
And a dozen at least to our young Commodore.
And though Britons may talk of their ruling the ocean,
And that sort of thing - by the Lord, I've a notion—
I'll bet all I'm worth - who takes it? who takes?
Though they're lords of the seas, we'll be lords of the Lakes.

Driving Saw-Logs on the Plover

By the 1850s the Maine woods were just about all chopped out, so the timber tigers shouldered their axes and headed west. Farm boys saw that there was more money to be made chopping than ploughing, although families did not always agree with the wisdom of their sons' choice.

Wisconsin

There walked on Plo – ver's shad – y banks One eve – ning last Ju – ly, A

moth – er of a shan – ty-boy, And dole – ful was her cry, Saying,

"God be with you, John – nie, Al – though you're far a – way Driv-ing

saw – logs on the Plo – ver, And you'll nev – er get your pay.

"O Johnnie, I gave you schooling,
I gave you a trade likewise;
You need not been a shanty-boy
Had you taken my advice.
You need not gone from your dear home
To the forest far away,
Driving saw-logs on the Plover,
And you'll never get your pay.

"O Johnnie, you were your father's hope,
Your mother's only joy.
Why is it that you ramble so,
My own, my darling boy?
What could induce you, Johnnie,
From your own dear home to stray,
Driving saw-logs on the Plover?
And you'll never get your pay.

"Why didn't you stay upon the farm,
And feed ducks and hens,
And drive the pigs and sheep each night
And put them in their pens?
Far better for you to help your dad
To cut his corn and hay
Than to drive saw-logs on the Plover,
And you'll never get your pay."

A log canoe came floating
Adown the quiet stream.
As peacefully it glided
As some young lover's dream.
A youth crept out upon the bank
And thus to her did say,
"Dear mother, I have jumped the game,
And I haven't got my pay.

"The boys called me a sucker
And a son-of-a-gun to boot.
I said to myself, 'O Johnnie,
It is time for you to scoot.'
I stole a canoe and started
Upon my weary way,
And now I have got home again,
But nary a cent of pay.

"Now all young men take this advice;
If e'er you wish to roam,
Be sure and kiss your mothers
Before you leave your home.
You had better work upon a farm
For half a dollar a day
Than to drive saw-logs on the Plover,
And you'll never get your pay."

On the Clearwater River. Courtesy of N.Y. Public Library Picture Collection.

Winning the Vote

The struggle for woman suffrage in America is actually older than our country. The first recorded demand for votes for women was made by Margaret Brent in Maryland in 1647. For the next 200 years, however, woman suffrage remained a minor issue as America fought the battle for national independence. The next important step forward in the woman suffrage movement came with the emergence of the great anti-slavery agitation of the 1830s and 1840s. The natural ideological affinity of the two causes was heightened by the active and leading role played by many women in the Abolitionist movement.... With the end of the Civil War...the suffrage movement took a gigantic leap ahead. It became apparent to the leading women's rights advocates that the key issue was suffrage. Accordingly, in 1869, Elizabeth Stanton and Susan B. Anthony helped to found the National Woman Suffrage Association under the inspiration of Lucy Stone and Julia Ward Howe.... At the great national suffrage conventions, at the historic parades and public demonstrations...the singing suffragettes chanted a melody of equal rights which unmistakably caught the ear of the nation.... (Sing Out, Vol. 6, No. 4, 1957)

Wisconsin

Words by Mrs. A. B. Smith (1912)
Published in Madison, Wisconsin

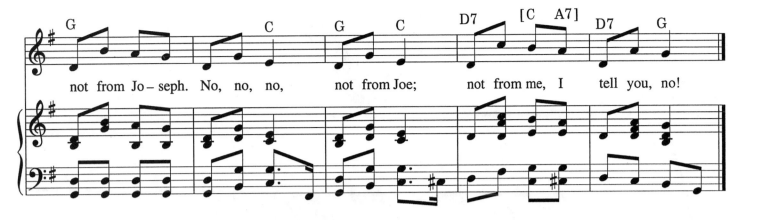

not from Jo – seph. No, no, no, not from Joe; not from me, I tell you, no!

Girls: Say, friend Joseph, why not we should vote as well as you?
Are there no problems in the State that need our wisdom, too?
We must pay our taxes same as you; as citizens be true,
And if some wicked thing we do, to jail we're sent by you.
Yes we are, same as you;
And you know it, don't you, Joseph?
Yes you do, yet you boast:
You'll not help us win the vote.

Boys: But dear women, can't you see, the home is your true sphere?
Just think of going to the polls perhaps two times a year.
You are wasting time you ought to use in sewing and at work,
Your home neglected all those hours; would you such duties shirk?
Help from Joe? Help from Joe?
If he knows it, not from Joseph;
No, no, no, not from Joe;
Not from me, I tell you, no!

Girls: Joseph, tell us something new – we're tired of that old song.
We'll sew the seams and cook the meals, to vote won't take us long.
We will help to clean house – the one too large for man to clean alone,
The State and Nation, don't you see, when we the vote have won.
Yes we will, and you'll help,
For you'll need our help, friend Joseph.
Yes you will, when we're in,
So you'd better help us win.

Boys: You're just right – how blind I've been, I ne'er had seen it thus;
'Tis true that taxes you must pay without a word of fuss.
You are subject to the laws men made, and yet no word or note
Can you sing out where it will count. I'll help you win the vote!
Yes, I will.

Girls: Thank you, Joe.

All: We'll together soon be voters.
Yes we will, if you'll all
Vote "Yes" at the polls next fall.

Heartland

Heartland

St. Louis, Missouri, 1872. Courtesy of N.Y. Public Library Picture Collection.

St. Louis Blues

When "St. Louis Blues" was written, the tango was the vogue. I tricked the dancers by arranging a tango introduction, breaking abruptly then into a low-down blues. My eyes swept the floor anxiously, then suddenly I saw the lightning strike. The dancers seemed electrified. Something within them came suddenly to life. An instinct that wanted so much to live, to fling its arms and to spread joy, took them by the heels. By this I was convinced that my new song was accepted.... Well, they say that life begins at 40 — I wouldn't know — but I was 40 the year "St. Louis Blues" was composed, and ever since then my life has...revolved around that composition. (Father of the Blues, An Autobiography by W. C. Handy, 1941)

Missouri

By W. C. Handy
(1914)

St. Lou-is wo-man, with her dia-mond rings pulls that man 'round by her a-pron strings. 'Twan't for pow-der and for store-bought hair, The man I love would not gone no-

way.

Jesse James

Between eight and nine o'clock yesterday morning Jesse James, the Missouri outlaw...was instantly killed by a boy twenty years old, named Robert Ford, at temporary residence on the corner of Thirteenth and Lafayette Streets in this city. In the light of all moral reasoning, the shooting was unjustifiable; but the law was vindicated, and the $10,000 reward offered by the state for the body of the brigand will doubtless go to the man who had the courage to draw a revolver on the notorious outlaw even when his back was turned, as in this case.... The shot [was] fatal, and all the bullets in Charlie's [Robert's brother] revolver, still directed at Jesse's head could not more effectively have determined the fate of the greatest bandit and freebooter that ever figured in the pages of a country's history.
(St. Joseph, Missouri, *Evening News*, April 3, 1882)

Missouri

Jes – se James was a lad who _ killed man – y a man, He robbed the Glen – dale

train. He _ stole from the rich and he gave to the poor, He'd a

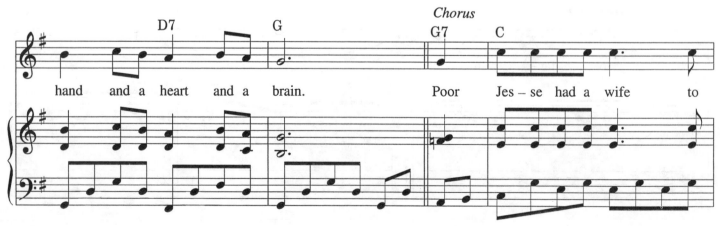

hand and a heart and a brain. Poor Jes – se had a wife to

mourn for his life, Three chil – dren they were brave; But that

dirt–y lit–tle cow–ard who shot Mis–ter How–ard has laid poor Jes–se in his grave.

It was Robert Ford, that dirty little coward,
I wonder how he does feel.
For he ate of Jesse's bread and he slept in Jesse's bed,
And he laid poor Jesse in his grave.   *Chorus*

How the people held their breath when they heard of
    Jesse's death.
And wondered how he ever came to die.
It was one of the gang, called Little Robert Ford
That shot poor Jesse on the sly.   *Chorus*

Jesse was a man, a friend to the poor,
He never would see a man suffer pain.
And with his brother Frank he robbed the Chicago bank,
And stopped the Glendale train.   *Chorus*

It was on a Wednesday night, the moon was shining bright,
They stopped the Glendale train.
And the people, they did say for many miles away,
It was robbed by Frank and Jesse James.   *Chorus*

They went to a crossing not very far from there,
And there they did the same.
With the agent on his knees, he delivered up the keys
To the outlaws, Frank and Jesse James.   *Chorus*

It was on a Saturday night, Jesse was at home,
Talking to his family brave.
Robert Ford came along like a thief in the night,
And laid poor Jesse in his grave.   *Chorus*

This song was made by Billy Gashade
As soon as the news did arrive.
He said there was no man with the law in his hand,
Who could take Jesse James while alive.   *Chorus*

Little Old Sod Shanty on the Plain

"I've got a little bet with the government," said the homesteader. "They're betting me I can't live here for five years, and I'm betting them I can." Under the terms of the Homestead Act of 1862, a man could claim 160 acres of land provided he worked and lived on his claim for five years.

Iowa

142

hin – ges are of leath – er and the win – dows have no glass, The boards they let the howl – ing bliz – zard in._____ You can

I rather like the novelty of living in this way,
Though my bill of fare isn't always of the Best,
But I'm happy as a clam on the land of Uncle Sam,
In my little old sod shanty in the West.   *Chorus*

But when I left my Eastern home, a bachelor so gay,
To try and win my way to wealth and fame,
I little thought I'd come down to burning twisted hay
In the little old sod shanty on my claim.   *Chorus*

My clothes are plastered o'er with dough, I'm looking like a fright,
And everything is scattered round the room;
But I wouldn't give the freedom that I have out in the West
For the table of the Eastern man's old home.   *Chorus*

Still, I wish that some kind-hearted girl would pity on me take,
And relieve me from the mess that I am in;
The angel, how I'd bless her if this her home she'd make
In the little old sod shanty on my claim.   *Chorus*

And if fate should bless us with now and then an heir
To cheer our hearts with honest pride of fame,
Oh, then we'd be contented for the toil that we had spent
In the little old sod shanty on our claim.   *Chorus*

When time enough had lapsed and all those little brats
To noble man and womanhood had grown,
It wouldn't seem half so lonely as round us we should look,
And we'd see the old sod shanty on our claim.   *Chorus*

143

If He's Good Enough For Lindy

(He's Good Enough For Me)

In May 1927, Charles Lindbergh flew his single-engine plane, *The Spirit of St. Louis*, across the Atlantic from New York to Paris — the first such flight in aviation history. The following year, Herbert Hoover of West Branch, Iowa, ran for the presidency of the United States. "Lucky Lindy" was a Hoover supporter, and his worldwide fame didn't do the presidential candidate any harm.

Iowa

Chorus (to the same melody as the verse):
If he's good enough for Lindy, he's good enough for me,
If he's good enough for Lindy, he's good enough for me,
If he's good enough for Lindy, he's good enough for me,
Herbert Hoover is the only man to be our nation's chief.

Charles Lindbergh flew his plane to France to see what he could see,
Now that he's back he's looking at our old country;
And what he has to say stands out in bold relief,
Herbert Hoover is the only man to be our nation's chief.   *Chorus*

Now you all remember Hoover, back in the war,
He saved us from the Kaiser, now he'll give us something more;
He'll serve as the President of the land of the free.
If he's good enough for Lindy, he's good enough for me.   *Chorus*

Herbert Hoover. Courtesy of N.Y. Public Library Picture Collection.

Kansas Fool

One worn-out farmer said: "In God we trusted, in Kansas we busted." His neighbor protested: " 'Them the Lord loveth, he chasteneth.' Well, he ain't done very much for us Kansas fellers but chasten us with sand storms, chinch bugs, cyclones, dry weather, blizzards, and grasshoppers. He must love us a turrible sight."

Kansas

146

twelve – cent corn gives me a – larm, And makes me want to sell my farm.

With abundant crops raised everywhere,
'Tis a mystery, I do declare;
Why, farmers all should fume and fret,
And why we are so deep in debt. *Chorus*

At first we made some money here,
With drouth and grasshoppers each year;
But now the interest that we pay
Soon takes our money all away. *Chorus*

The bankers followed us out west,
And did in mortgages invest;
They looked ahead and shrewdly planned,
And soon they'll have our Kansas land. *Chorus*

A Pioneer Family on the Kansas Prairie. Courtesy of N.Y. Public Library Picture Collection.

147

Quantrell

William C. Quantrill ("Quantrell") was a Confederate border irregular during the Civil War. Trained for guerilla warfare in Kansas and Missouri, he and his "border bandits" — including Jesse and Frank James and Cole Younger — soon realized that "the law of the gun" had placed them in a privileged position in the wild frontier during and after the war. On August 21, 1863, after sacking several small towns along the Kansas–Missouri border, he rode his men into Lawrence, where they burned down some 200 buildings and killed over 150 residents.

Kansas

Come all you bold rob – bers and o – pen your ears, of

Quan – trell the lion – heart you quick – ly shall hear; With his

band of bold raid – ers in dou – ble – quick time, They

came to burn Law – rence just o – ver the line

148

Chorus:

All routing and shouting and giving the yell,
Like so many demons just raised up from Hell,
The boys they were drunken with powder and wine,
And came to burn Lawrence just over the line.

They came to burn Lawrence, they came not to stay,
They rode in one morning at breaking of day,
Their guns were a-waving and horses a-foam,
And Quantrell a-riding his famous big roan.　　*Chorus*

They came to burn Lawrence, they came not to stay.
Jim Lane he was up at the break of the day;
He saw them a-coming and got in a fright,
Then crawled in a corncrib to get out of sight.　　*Chorus*

Oh, Quantrell's a fighter, a bold-hearted boy,
A brave man or woman he'll never annoy,
He'd take from the wealthy and give to the poor,
For brave men there's never a bolt to his door.　　*Chorus*

Massacre at Lawrence, Kansas, by Quantrill's Guerrillas. Courtesy of N.Y. Public Library Picture Collection.

Cole Younger

On September 7, 1876, the Younger brothers, Cole and Bob, and the James brothers, Jesse and Frank, rode into Stillwater, Minnesota, with their gang. They had their "eye on the Northfield Bank," but unlike so many of their previous holdups and robberies, this time the good people of Stillwater were ready and waiting for them. In a violent shoot-out, two members of the gang were killed and Bob Younger was wounded. Two weeks later Cole and Bob were captured. The James boys got clean away.

Minnesota

'Tis of a bold high robbery, a story I will tell,
Of a California miner who unto us fell,
We robbed him of his money and bid him go his way,
For which I will be sorry until my dying day.

And then we started homeward, when Brother Bob did say,
"Now, Cole, we'll buy fast horses and on them ride away;
We'll ride to avenge our father's death and try to win the prize,
We'll fight those anti-guerillas until the day we die."

And then we rode towards Texas, that good old Lone Star state,
But on Nebraska's prairies the James boys we did meet,
With knives and guns and pistols we all sat down to play,
A-drinkin' of good whisky, boys, to pass the time away.

A Union Pacific railway train was the next we did surprise,
And the crimes done by our bloody hands bring tears into my eyes,
The engineer and the fireman killed, the conductor escaped alive,
And now their bones lie mouldering beneath Nebraska's skies.

Then we saddled horses, north-westward we did go,
To the God-forsaken country called Minnesot-i-o,
I had my eye on the Northfield Bank, when brother Bob did say,
"Now Cole, if you undertake the job, you'll surely rue the day."

But I stationed out my pickets and up to the bank did go,
And there upon the counter I struck my fatal blow.
"Just hand us over your money and make no further delay,
We are the famous Younger boys, we spend no time in play."

The cashier, being as true as steel, refused our noted band,
'Twas Jesse James that pulled the trigger that killed this noble man.
We run for life, for death was near, four hundred on our trail,
We soon were overtaken, and landed safe in jail.

I am a noted highwayman, Cole Younger is my name,
My crimes and depredations have brought my name to shame,
And now in the Stillwater Jail I lie, a-wearin' my life away,
Two James boys live to tell the tale of that sad and fatal day.

Bob, Cole, and Jim Younger. Courtesy of N.Y. Public Library Picture Collection.

The Shantyman's Life

The statue of the mythical lumberman Paul Bunyan and his blue ox, Babe, is to be found in Bemedji, Minnesota. Paul Bunyan is the logger's equivalent of the steel driver's John Henry. When it came to cutting down timber and hauling it out of the woods, no man or beast could touch Paul and Babe. This song comes from Bemedji.

Minnesota

Oh, a shan – ty – man's life is a wear – i – some life, al – though some think it void of care, _____ Swing – ing an ax from _____ morn – ing till night, in the midst of the for – ests so drear. _____ Ly – ing in the shan – ty _____ bleak and _____ cold while the

cold — storm-y win-try winds___ blow, And as soon as the day – light
does ap – pear, to the wild woods___ we must go.

Oh, the cook rises up in the middle of the night saying, "Hurrah, brave boys, it's day."
Broken slumbers ofttimes are passed as the cold winter night whiles away.
Had we rum, wine or beer our spirits for to cheer as the days so lonely do dwine,
Or a glass of any shone while in the woods alone for to cheer up our troubled minds.

But when spring it does set in, double hardships then begin, when the waters are piercing cold,
And our clothes are dripping wet and fingers benumbed, and our pike-poles we scarcely can hold.
Betwixt rocks, shoals and sands give employment to all hands our well-banded raft for to steer,
And the rapids that we run, oh, they seem to us but fun, for we're void of all slavish fear.

Oh, a shanty lad is the only lad I love, and I never will deny the same.
My heart doth scorn these conceited farmer boys who think it a disgraceful name.
They may boast about their farms, but my shanty-boy has charms so far, far surpassing them all,
Until death it doth us part he shall enjoy my heart, let his riches be great or small.

The Kinkaiders

In an effort to attract farmers to Nebraska, Moses P. Kinkaid, congressman from the Sixth District, 1903–1919, introduced a bill for 640-acre homesteads. He was hailed as a benefactor of the sandhill region.

Nebraska

The corn we raise is our delight,
The melons, too, are out of sight.
Potatoes grown are extra fine
And can't be beat in any clime. *Chorus*

The peaceful cows in pastures dream,
And furnish us with golden cream,
So I shall keep my Kinkaid home
And never far away shall roam.

Final Chorus:

Then let us all with hearts sincere
Thank him for what has brought us here,
And for the homestead law he made,
This noble Moses P. Kinkaid.

Homestead in Nebraska, 1900. Courtesy of N.Y. Public Library Picture Collection.

The Texas Cowboy In Nebraska

The drives long up the trail occupied months, and called for sleepless vigilance and tireless activity both day and night. When at last a shipping point was reached, the cattle marketed or loaded on the cars, the cowboys were paid off. The music, the dancing, the click of the roulette balls in the saloons, invited; the lure of the crimson lights was irresistible. Drunken orgies, reactions to months of toil, deprivation, and loneliness on the ranch and on the trail, brought death to many a crazed buckaroo. (Alan Lomax and Joshua Berrett in the introduction to the 1986 edition of *Cowboy Songs and Other Frontier Ballads* by John Lomax, first published in 1910)

Nebraska

Oh, I am a Tex – as cow–boy, I'm far a – way from home; If
ev–er I get back to Tex – as, I nev – er – more will roam. Ne –
bras–ka is too cold for me and the win – ters are too long; Be –
fore the round – ups do be–gin, Our mon – ey is all gone.

Take this old hen-skin bedding, too thin to keep me warm,
I nearly freeze to death, my boys, whenever there's a storm.
And take this old tarpoleon, too thin to shield my frame,
I got it down in Nebraska a-dealin' a monte game.

Now, to win these fancy leggins I'll have enough to do;
They cost me twenty dollars the day that they were new.
I have an outfit on the Mussel Shell, but that I'll never see,
The less I get to represent the Circle or D.T.

I've worked up in Nebraska where the grass grows ten feet high,
And the cattle are such rustlers that they seldom ever die;
I've worked up in the sand hills and down upon the Platte,
Where the cowboys are good fellows and the cattle always fat.

I've traveled lots of country – Nebraska's hills of sand,
Down through the Indian Nation, and up the Rio Grande;
But the Bad Lands of Nebraska are the worst I ever seen,
The cowboys are all tenderfeet and the dogies are too lean.

If you want to see some bad lands, go over on the Dry;
You will bog down in the coulees where the mountains reach the sky.
A tenderfoot to lead you who never knows the way,
You are playing in the best of luck if you eat more than once a day.

Your grub is bread and bacon and coffee black as ink;
The water is so full of alkali it is hardly fit to drink,
They will wake you in the morning before the break of day,
And send you on a circle a hundred miles away.

All along the River Platte 'tis cold the year around;
You will surely get consumption by sleeping on the ground.
Work in Nebraska is six months in the year;
When all your bills are settled there is nothing left for beer.

Work down in Texas is all the year around;
You will never get consumption by sleeping on the ground.
Come all you Texas cowboys and warning take from me,
And do not go to Nebraska to spend your money free.
But stay at home in Texas where work lasts the year round,
And you will never catch consumption by sleeping on the ground.] *Repeat last 8 measures*

Dakota Land

In...the Dakotas...the land was rich, but nature was a savage adversary, and it took all a man's strength and will to draw his sustenance from this unplowed earth. Laughing at themselves, they took an old hymn called "Beulah Land" and fashioned it into a mocking commentary on their own gullibility. (*Songs of the Great American West* by Irwin Silber, 1967)

North Dakota

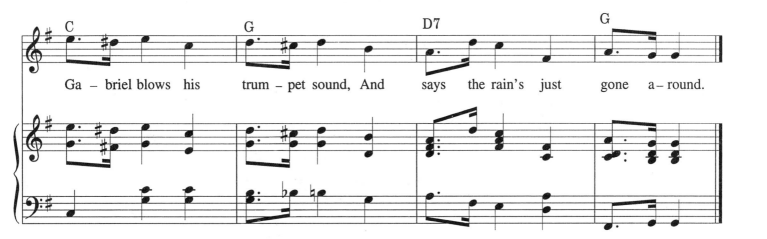

Ga – briel blows his trum – pet sound, And says the rain's just gone a – round.

We've reached the land of hills and stones
Where all is strewn with buffalo bones.
O buffalo bones, bleached buffalo bones,
I seem to hear your sighs and moans.   *Chorus*

We have no wheat, we have no oats,
We have no corn to feed our shoats;
Our chickens are so very poor
They beg for crumbs outside the door.   *Chorus*

Our horses are of bronco race;
Starvation stares them in the face.
We do not live, we only stay;
We are too poor to get away.   *Chorus*

Courtesy of N.Y. Public Library Picture Collection.

The Swede From North Dakota

Scandinavian immigrants headed for the upper Midwestern states by the thousands. Anxiously awaiting the next ship over, the Swedes sang:

We must cross the salty waves,
Brothers get in motion,
And we'll reach America
Far across the ocean.

When they arrived in the "promised land," they often sang a different tune:

In North Dakota (I'll be darn),
The "wise guy" sleeps in "hoosier's" barn.
Then hoosier breaks into his snore,
And yells, "It's quarter after four!"

North Dakota

I bin a Swade from Nort' Da–ko–ta, Work–on a farm–stead 'bout two yare;
Tank I go to Min–ne–so–ta, Go to Min–ne–ap–o–lis to see great fair.

Walking round the street in Saint Paul
Ain't seen any feller anywhere
So I jump on streetcar to Minneapolis
Bet your life lots Swede men there.

I buy me a suit, I buy me a bottle,
Dress me up way out of sight;
Yump on the tail of a Yim Hill wagon
Yesus Chreest, I feel for fight!

I go down to Seven Corners
Where Salvation Army play.
One dem vomans come to me;
This is what dat voman say.

She say, "Will you work for Yesus?"
I say, "How much Yesus pay?"
She say, "Yesus don't pay nothing."
I say, "I won't work today."

So I go back to North Dakota
Get a job on farm somewhere
And I say to all Swede fellers
They can go to heck with the big State Fair.

Just Before The Drawing, Sweetheart

The Populist party was a reform party of farmers and workers created after the Civil War and having its greatest strength between 1890 and 1910. Populist songs tended to be parodies of well-known songs. This tried-and-true technique virtually guaranteed that people would be able to sing these new versions upon first hearing. George Root's Civil War classic "Just Before the Battle, Mother" lent itself perfectly to a re-write. Its unknown author expresses the Populist dream of a piece of land and a chance for a better life with one's loved ones.

South Dakota

Music by George F. Root

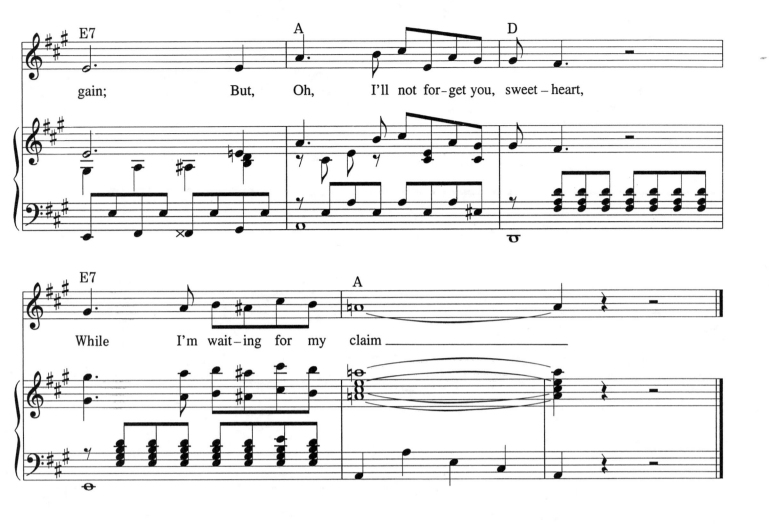

gain;   But,   Oh,   I'll not for-get you, sweet – heart,

While   I'm wait – ing for   my   claim

Way out here in Dewey County,
Way out here upon the plains,
Way out here upon my homestead,
Where they say it never rains.
Just before the drawing, sweetheart,
Many they are coming here;
They have left their homes and fam'lies,
They have left their sweethearts dear. *Chorus*

They are coming for the drawing,
They are hoping for a home,
Where they'll take their own dear loved ones,
And no more will ever roam.
Now, my darling watch the paper,
And if you should see my name,
You will know we have a homestead,
You will know we have a claim. *Chorus*

Then, my sweetheart, you get ready,
Then to Pierre you may come.
We'll go in a prairie schooner,
To our Dewey County home.
Way out here in Dewey County,
Where they say it never rains,
Our sod shanty is waiting
Our home upon the plains. *Chorus*

The Dreary Black Hills

"The Dreary Black Hills" first appeared as a broadside around 1875, "as sung by Dick Brown." At that time, there was no boundary between Wyoming and Dakota Territory, and the Black Hills were in the Lakota territory. Speculation has it that Dick Brown, who was a banjo player and singer, was the "Deadwood Dick" who was described in stories as a notorious stagecoach robber. In reality, he arrived in the Black Hills from Cheyenne in 1875 and performed at the Melodeon, a saloon and gambling hall in Deadwood.

South Dakota

164

Chorus:
Don't go away, stay at home if you can,
Stay away from that city they call it Cheyenne,
Where the blue waters roll, and Comanche Bills,
They will lift up your hair, on the dreary Black Hills.

I got to Cheyenne, no gold could I find,
I thought of the lunch route I'd left far behind:
Through rain, hail, and snow, frozen plumb to the gills,
They call me the orphan of the dreary Black Hills. *Chorus*

Kind friend, to conclude, my advice I'll unfold,
Don't go to the Black Hills a-hunting for gold;
Railroad speculators their pockets you'll fill
By taking a trip to those dreary Black Hills.

Final Chorus:
Don't go away, stay at home if you can,
Stay away from that city, they call it Cheyenne,
For old Sitting Bull or Comanche Bills
They will take off your scalp on the dreary Black Hills.

A Miner's Log Cabin in the Black Hills of South Dakota. Courtesy of N.Y. Public Library Picture Collection.

Southwest

Southwest

Guthrie, Oklahoma, 1893. Courtesy of N.Y. Public Library Picture Collection.

Pretty Boy Floyd

Nineteen thirty-four was a bad year for criminal fugitives. In that year, FBI special agents were authorized to carry firearms and make arrests, with the result that three of the most notorious outlaws met their deaths while resisting arrest: John Dillinger, Lester Gillis (alias Baby Face Nelson), and Charles Arthur ("Pretty Boy") Floyd. While Dillinger and Nelson were universally regarded as "bad men," a Jesse James–Robin Hood aura surrounded the deeds of Floyd.

Oklahoma

By Woody Guthrie

If you'll gath–er 'round me, chil–dren, A sto–ry I will tell,___ A–bout Pret–ty Boy Floyd, the out–law, Ok–la–ho–ma knew him well.

It was in the town of Shawnee,
On a Saturday afternoon,
His wife beside him in the wagon,
And into town they rode.

A deputy sheriff approached him
In a manner rather rude,
With vulgar words of anger
Which Mis' Floyd overheard.

Pretty Boy grabbed a log chain,
The deputy grabbed his gun;
And in the fight that followed
He laid that deputy down.

The outlaw took to the country
To live a life of shame;
Every crime in Oklahoma
Was added to his name.

He took to the trees and timber
Along the river shore,
And Pretty Boy found a welcome
At many a farmer's door.

There's many a starving family
The same old story told
How the outlaw paid the mortgage
And saved their little home.

Others tell you of a stranger
Who came to beg a meal,
And underneath the napkin
Left a thousand dollar bill.

In Oklahoma City
Upon a Christmas Day,
A whole carload of groceries
Came with a note to say:

"You say that I'm an outlaw,
You say that I'm a thief;
Well, here's a Christmas dinner
For the families on relief."

Now as through this world I've wandered,
I've seen many kinds of men;
Some will rob you with a six-gun,
And some with a fountain pen.

As through this world you wander,
As through this world you roam,
You won't never see an outlaw
Drive a family from their home.

Oklahoma Hills

In the summer of 1937, cousins Jack and Woody Guthrie were on the air on radio station KFVD in Los Angeles as *The Oklahoma and Woody Show*. They sang mostly cowboy songs, which were all the rage in that era of "the singing cowboy." In September Jack left the program, and Woody invited Maxine Crissman ("Lefty Lou") to join him on the air. They sang duets and were a great success. It was about that time that Woody began writing his own songs. "Oklahoma Hills" was one of those early compositions, and it received its first performance on KFVD. When Jack recorded the song for Capitol records in 1945, he was at first credited with its composition, an "oversight" which was corrected in a 1948 Capitol album in which Jack and Woody share credit as co-writers.

Oklahoma

By Jack Guthrie and Woody Guthrie

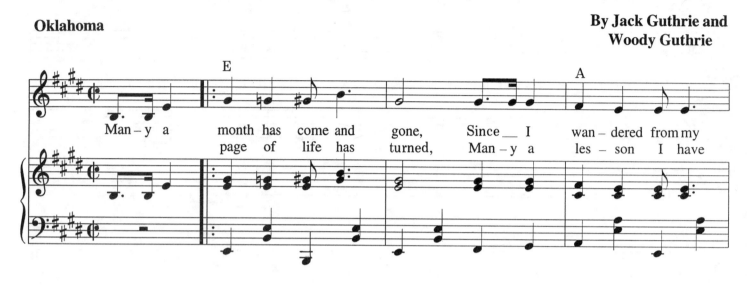

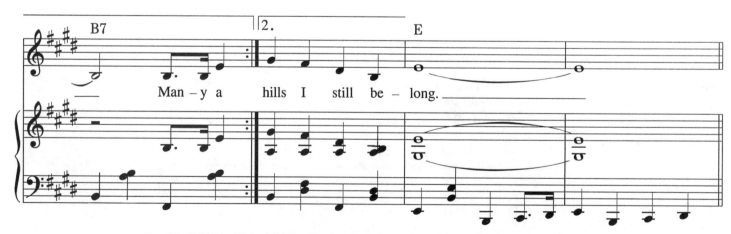

But as I sit here today,
Many miles I am away
From the place I rode my pony through the draw;
While the oak and black-jack trees
Kiss the playful prairie breeze,
In those Oklahoma hills where I was born.   *Chorus*

Now as I turn life a page,
To the land of the Great Osage,
In those Oklahoma hills where I was born;
While the black oil it rolls and flows,
And the snow-white cotton grows
In those Oklahoma hills where I was born. *Chorus*

Hell in Arizona

Arizona booster: "Arizona needs only water and climate to make it a paradise." Skeptical listener: "Yes, that's all hell needs, too."

Arizona

The De – vil was giv – en per – mis – sion one day To se-

lect him a land for his own spe – cial sway; So he

hunt – ed a – round for a month ___ or more, And ___

fussed and fumed ___ and ter – rib – ly swore.

He at last was delighted a country to view
Where the prickly pear and the mesquite grew.
With a survey brief, without further excuse,
He stood on the bank of the Santa Cruz.

He saw there were some improvements to make,
For he felt his own reputation at stake.
An idea struck him, and he swore by his horns
To make a complete vegetation of thorns.

He studded the land with the prickly pear,
And scattered the cactus everywhere;
The Spanish dagger, sharp-pointed and tall,
And at last the chollas to outstick them all.

He filled the river with sand 'til 'twas almost dry,
And poisoned the land with alkali;
And promised himself on its slimy brink
To control all who from it should drink.

He saw there was one improvement to make,
So he imported the scorpion, tarantula, and snake,
That all that might come to this country to dwell,
Would be sure to think it was almost hell.

He fixed the heat at a hundred and 'leven,
And banished forever the moisture from heaven;
And remarked as he heard his furnaces roar
That the heat might reach five hundred more.

And after he fixed things so thorny and well
He said, "I'll be damned if this don't beat hell."
Then he flapped his wings and away he flew
And vanished from earth in a blaze of blue.

Arizona Rangers. Courtesy of N.Y. Public Library Picture Collection.

Billy Venero

In the frontier days, when there were Indians to be subdued by bloodshed and fortunes to be made by ruthlessness, cowboys wore two guns and lived by a code of violence. But there was considerable gentility, even on the frontier.... Respect for good women was a cardinal principle of morality, a tradition which still operates with such force that all cowboys apologize at saying "damn" before a lady. (Singing Cowboys by Margaret Larkin, 1931)

Arizona

In an A – ri – zo – na town one day, Bil – ly Ve – ne – ro heard them say, That a band of A – pa – che In – dians _____ were on the trail of death. Heard them tell of mur – der done, Three men killed at Rock – y Run. "They're in dan – ger at the Cow – Ranch," _____ Said Ve – ne – ro un – der breath.

Cow-Ranch forty miles away,
Was a little spot that lay
In a deep and shady valley
Of the mighty wilderness.
Half a score of homes were there,
And in one a maiden fair,
Held the heart of Billy Venero,
Billy Venero's little Bess.

So no wonder he grew pale,
When he heard the cowboy's tale,
Of the men that he'd seen murdered
The day before at Rocky Run.
"Sure as there's a God above,
I will save the girl I love;
By my love for little Bessie,
I will see that something's done."

Not a moment he delayed
When his brave resolve was made.
"Why man," his comrades told him
When they heard his daring plan,
"You are riding straight to death."
But he answered, "Save your breath.
I may never reach the Cow-Ranch,
But I'll do the best I can."

As he crossed the alkali
All his thoughts flew on ahead
To the little band at Cow-Ranch
Thinking not of danger near;
With his quirt's unceasing whirl
And the jingle of his spurs
Little Chapo bore the cowboy
O'er the far away frontier.

Lower and lower sank the sun;
He drew rein at Rocky Run.
"Here those men met death, my Chapo,"
And he stroked the glossy mane.
"So shall those we go to warn,
'Ere the coming of the morn.
If we fail – God help my Bessie,"
And he started on again.

Sharp and clear a rifle shot
Woke the echoes of that spot.
"I am wounded," cried Venero
As he swayed from side to side.
"While there's life there's always hope,
Slowly onward I will lope.
If we fail to reach the Cow-Ranch
Bessie Lee shall know I tried."

"I will save her yet," he cried,
"Bessie Lee shall know I tried,"
And for her sake then he halted
In the shadow of a hill.
From his chapareras he took
With weak hands a little book.
Tore a blank leaf from its pages,
Saying, "This shall be my will."

From a limb a pen he broke,
And he dipped his pen of oak
In the warm blood that was spurting
From a wound above his heart.
"Rouse," he wrote, "before too late,
Apache warriors lie in wait.
Good-bye, God bless you darling,"
And he felt the cold tears start.

Then he made his message fast,
Love's first message and its last,
To the saddle horn he tied it,
And his lips were white with pain.
"Take this message, if not me,
Straight to little Bessie Lee."
Then he tied himself to the saddle,
And he gave his horse the rein.

Just at dusk a horse of brown,
Wet with sweat came panting down
The little lane at Cow-Ranch,
Stopped in front of Bessie's door.
But the cowboy was asleep,
And his slumbers were so deep
Little Bess could never wake him
Though she tried for evermore.

You have heard the story told
By the young and by the old,
Away down yonder at the Cow-Ranch
The night the Apaches came.
Of that sharp and bloody fight,
How the chief fell in the fight,
And the panic-stricken warriors
When they heard Venero's name.

Sung to last 4 measures:
And the heavens and earth between
Keep a little flower so green,
That little Bess has planted,
'Ere they laid her by his side.

Billy the Kid

William H. Bonney, who came to be known as "Billy the Kid," was born, improbably enough, on Rivington Street on the Lower East Side of Manhattan on November 23, 1859. He moved west with his parents and eventually found himself in Silver City, New Mexico. It was there he established his "rep" at the age of 12 by shooting down a man who had insulted his mother. Over the next ten years his reputation as a cold-blooded, psychopathic killer grew and grew until he was shot to death by his former friend, Sheriff Pat Garrett, on July 14, 1881. Then legend took over and attempted to portray him as a folk hero, a guardian of the poor and a defier of authority. However, the grim facts of his life as a gun-for-hire murderer do not really allow for any excessive romanticization of this outlaw.

New Mexico

I'll sing you a true song of Bil – ly the Kid; Sing of the des – per – ate deeds that he did way out in New Mex – i – co long, long a – go, Where a man's on – ly friend was his old for – ty four.

When Billy the Kid was a very young lad,
In old Silver City he went to the bad.
Way out in the West with a gun in his hand,
At the age of twelve years he killed his first man.

Young Mexican maidens play guitars and sing
Songs about Billy, their boy bandit king,
How there's a young man who had reached his sad end –
Had a notch on his pistol for twenty-one men.

It was on the same night when poor Billy died,
He said to his friends, "I'm not satisfied.
There are twenty-one men I have put bullets through,
Sheriff Pat Garrett must make twenty-two."

Now this is how Billy the Kid met his fate,
The bright moon was shining, the hour was late.
Shot down by Pat Garrett who once was his friend,
The young outlaw's life had now reached its sad end.

Now there's many a lad with a face fine and fair,
Who starts out in life with a chance to be square,
But just like poor Billy they wander astray,
They lose their life in the very same way.

New Mexico During the 1800s. Courtesy of N.Y. Public Library Picture Collection.

O Sleep, My Little Baby

Duérmete, Niño Lindo

This is a lullaby from the Christmas pageant *Los Pastores,* introduced by the Spanish missionaries into New Mexico during the 16th century. When the Spaniards were driven out of New Spain in 1821, many parishes were left without *padres;* but *Los Pastores* and other folk dramas and songs were spread into Spanish-speaking communities throughout the Southwest. The pageant is still performed in communities and schools.

New Mexico

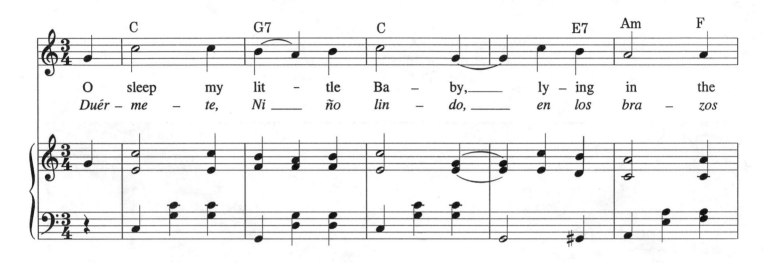

O sleep my lit - tle Ba - by,____ ly - ing in the
Duér - me - te, Ni ____ ño lin - do, ____ en los bra - zos

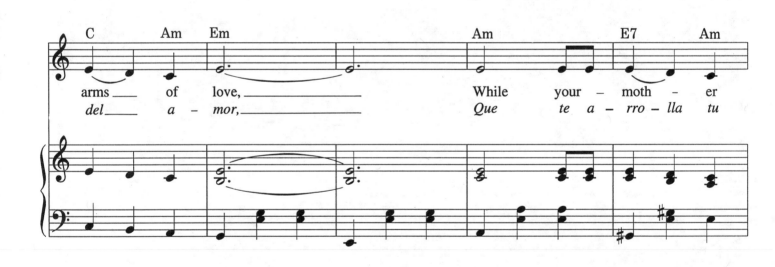

arms ____ of love,____ While your - moth - er
del ____ a - mor,____ Que te a - rro - lla tu

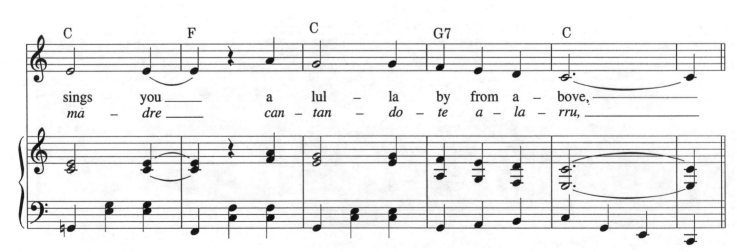

sings you ____ a lul - la by from a - bove,____
ma - dre ____ can - tan - do - te a - la - rru,____

Chorus

A – la rru, _____ a la me, _____ a – la – rru, _____ a – la me, _____ A – la – rru, a – la – rru, a – la – me. _____

Oh, have no fear of Herod,
He can do no harm to you,
Here in the arms of your mother
While she sings alarru.   *Chorus*

No temas a Herodes,
Que nada te ha de hacer.
En los brazos de tu madre,
Nadie te ha de ofender.   Chorus

Valencia, New Mexico. Courtesy of N.Y. Public Library Picture Collection.

177

The Galveston Flood

On September 8, 1900, a hurricane with a wind velocity of 135 miles per hour struck Galveston. The winds blew steadily for 18 hours, sending enormous waves from the Gulf of Mexico sweeping across a large part of the city. More than 8,000 buildings were destroyed or damaged; loss of life was estimated at about 5,000.

Texas

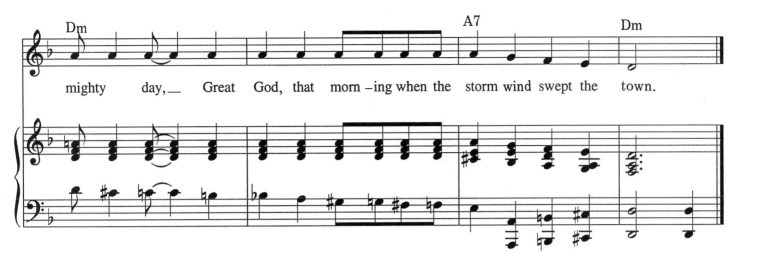

mighty day,— Great God, that morn –ing when the storm wind swept the town.

There was a seawall there in Galveston,
To keep the waters down;
But the high tide from the ocean, God,
Put water into the town. *Chorus*

The waters, like some river,
Came rushing to and fro;
Seen my father drowning, God,
I watched my mother go. *Chorus*

Well, the trumpets gave them warning,
You'd better leave this place;
But they never meant to leave their homes
Till death was in their face. *Chorus*

The sea began to rollin',
The ships they could not land,
Heard a captain crying, "God,
Please save this drowning man!" *Chorus*

Sea Wall at Galveston, Texas. Courtesy of N.Y. Public Library Picture Collection.

The Streets of Laredo

One day as I strolled down by the Royal Arsenal,
Cold was the morning and wet was the day,
When who did I meet but one of my shipmates,
Wrapped up in flannel, yet colder than clay.

Then beat the drum lowly,
Sound the dead march as you carry him on.
Take him to the churchyard and throw the dirt o'er him,
For he's a young sailor cut down in his prime.

So begins the old English ballad "The Young Sailor Cut Down in His Prime," which crossed the Atlantic with other young sailors, where it eventually found a new home among the cowboys on the banks of the Rio Grande.

Texas

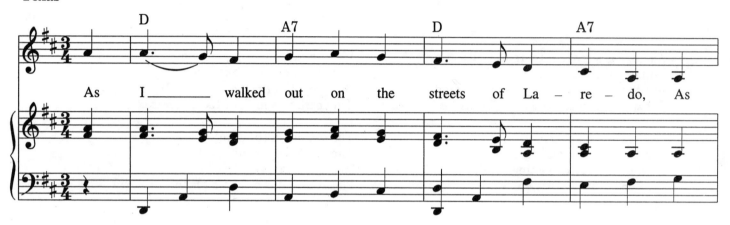

As I_____ walked out on the streets of La – re – do, As

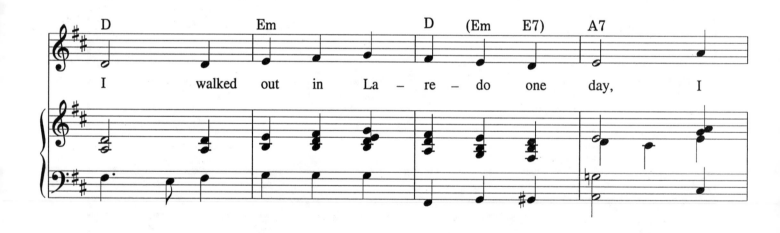

I walked out in La – re – do one day, I

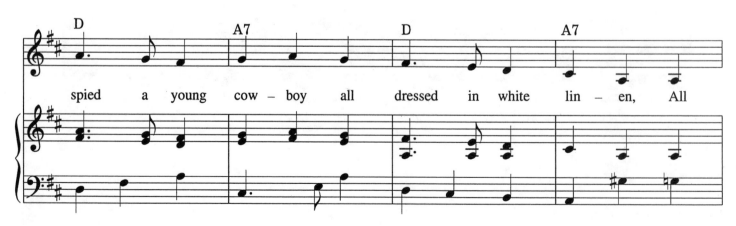

spied a young cow – boy all dressed in white lin – en, All

180

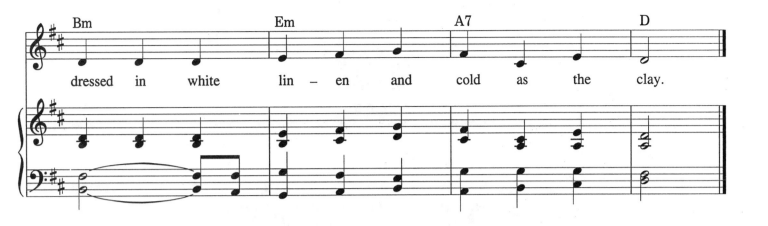

dressed in white lin – en and cold as the clay.

"I see by your outfit that you are a cowboy,"
These words he did say as I proudly stepped by,
"Come sit down beside me and hear my sad story,
Got shot in the breast and I know I must die.

" 'Twas once in the saddle I used to go dashing,
'Twas once in the saddle I used to go gay;
'Twas first to drinkin', and then to card-playing,
Got shot in the breast and I'm dying today.

"Let six jolly cowboys come carry my coffin,
Let six pretty ladies come carry my pall;
Throw bunches of roses all over my coffin,
Throw roses to deaden the clods as they fall.

"Oh beat the drum slowly, and play the fife lowly,
And play the dead march as you carry me along,
Take me to the green valley and lay the earth o'er me,
For I'm a poor cowboy and I know I've done wrong."

Oh we beat the drum slowly and we played the fife lowly,
And bitterly wept as we carried him along,
For we all loved our comrade, so brave, young and handsome,
We all loved our comrade although he done wrong.

Courtesy of N.Y. Public Library Picture Collection.

Mountain

Mountain

Creede, Colorado. Courtesy of N.Y. Public Library Picture Collection.

Tying a Knot in the Devil's Tail

Encounters with the devil are a recurrent theme in folklore and folk songs around the world. Each culture deals with Old Nick in its own way. The cowboys used the rope and the branding iron.

Nevada

Way up high in the Hum-boldt-peaks, Where the yel-low pines grow tall,
San-dy Bob and Bus-ter Jiggs had a round-up camp last fall.

They took their horses and their runnin' irons,
And maybe a dog or two,
And they 'lowed they'd brand all the long-eared calves
That came within their view.

Well, many a long-eared dogie
That didn't hush up by day,
Had his long ears whittled and his old hide scorched
In a most artistic way.

Then one fine day said Buster Jiggs,
As he throwed his cigo down:
"I'm tired of cow biography,
And I 'lows I'm goin' to town."

They saddles up and they hits them a lope,
Fer it weren't no sight of a ride,
An' them was the days when an old cow hand
Could oil up his old insides.

They starts her out at the Kentucky bar
At the head of the whisky row,
And they winds her up at the Depot House,
Some forty drinks below.

They sets her up and turns her around,
And goes her the other way,
And to tell you the Lord forsaken truth
Them boys got drunk that day.

Well, as they was a-headin' back to camp
And packin' a pretty good load,
Who should they meet but the Devil, himself,
Come prancin' down the road.

Now the Devil he said: "You cowboy skunks,
You better go hunt your hole,
'Cause I come up from the hell's rim-rock
To gather in your souls."

Said Buster Jiggs: "Now we're just from town
An' feelin' kind o' tight,
And you ain't gonna get no cowboy souls
Without some kind of a fight."

So he punched a hole in his old throw rope
And he slings her straight and true,
And he roped the Devil right around the horns
He takes his dallies* true.

Old Sandy Bob was a reata†-man
With his rope all coiled up neat,
But he shakes her out and he builds him a loop
And he roped the Devil's hind feet.

They threw him down on the desert ground,
While the irons was a-gettin' hot,
They cropped and swallow-forked his ears
And branded him up a lot.

And they pruned him up with a dehorning saw
And knotted his tail for a joke,
Rode off and left him bellowing there,
Necked up to a lilac-jack

Well, if you ever travel in the Humboldt peaks
And you hear one helluva wail,
You'll know it's nothin' but the Devil, himself,
Raisin' hell about the knots in his tail.

turns of the rope around the saddle horn † lasso

In Rawhide
Where Young And Old Are Finding Gold

When this song was published in 1908, Rawhide was a wide-open boomtown. During the glory years of 1907 and 1908, an estimated 10,000 people swarmed into the area, attracted by great strikes such as the Grutt Hill Mine and Stingaree Gulch. Rawhide's one church did the best it could to save the poor sinners from the 90 saloons, whose splendor was said to have rivaled San Franciso's Barbary Coast. Most of the town was destroyed in a fire that raced through the tents and wooden buildings on September 4, 1908.

Nevada

Words by Fred Jones
Music by Glenn W. Ashley

186

And Shaf-fer's Lease! Will won-ders cease? It beats the fa-mous Mo-hawk. _____ Out on the street In crowds you meet, 'Tis told the same as in-side. _____ There's gold ga-lore in na-ture's store, Be-neath the town of Raw-hide. _____

Root Hog Or Die

When word of the discovery of gold around Pike's Peak filtered back east in the spring of 1859, a great surge of humanity, reminiscent of the forty-niners who had headed for California ten years earlier, hit the trail for Colorado. There was gold, all right, but "them thar hills" kept most of it to themselves, defying the prospectors' puny picks and pans. It was only after the big operators moved in with heavy machinery that great fortunes would be blasted out of the rock. So most of the famous "Pike's Peak or Bust" signs had to be painted over with a new legend: "Busted, by Gosh!"

Colorado

Way out up-on the Platte, ___ near Pike's peak we were told, There by a lit-tle dig-ging, we could get a pile of gold. So we bun-dled up our cloth-ing, re-solved at least to try And tempt old Mad-am For-tune, root ___ hog or die.

So we traveled across the country, and we got upon the ground,
But cold weather was ahead, the first thing we found.
We built our shanties on the ground, resolved in spring to try,
To gather up the dust and slugs, root hog, or die.

Speculation is the fashion even at this early stage,
And corner lots and big hotels appear to be the rage.
The emigration's bound to come, and to greet them we will try,
Big pig, little pig, root hog, or die.

Let shouts resound, the cup pass 'round, we all came for gold,
The politicians are all gas, the speculators sold.
The "scads" are all we want, and to get them we will try,
Big pig, little pig, root hog, or die.

Surveyors now are at their work, laying off the towns,
And some will be of low degree, and some of high renown.
They don't care a jot nor tittle who do buy
The corner lots, or any lots, root hog, or die.

The doctors are among us, you can find them where you will,
They say their trade it is to cure, I say it is to kill;
They'll dose you and they'll physic you, until they make you sigh,
And their powders and their lotions make you root hog, or die.

The next in turn comes lawyers, a precious set are they,
In the public dairy they drink the milk, their clients drink the whey.
A cunning set these fellows are, they'll sap you till you're dry,
And never leave you will they have to root hog, or die.

A preacher now is all we want, to make us all do good;
But at present, there's no lack of spiritual food.
The kind I refer to will make you laugh or cry,
And it's real name is Taos, root hog, or die.

I have finished now my song, or if you please, my ditty,
And that it was not shorter is about the only pity.
And now that I have had my say, don't say I've told a lie,
For the subject I've touched will make us root hog, or die.

Ludlow Massacre

In 1913 the coal fields of southern Colorado were only nominally in the United States. In every practical sense they were autonomous states in which every function of government was controlled by the operators. Houses, stores, churches, streets, towns, land, were company-owned. Company guards policed the streets and enforced the law of the operators.... Miners were paid not in United States currency, but in company scrip, in defiance of the law.... It is no surprise in view of such conditions...the miners struck on September 23, 1913.... The real point of contention was the union. (American Folksongs of Protest by John Greenway, 1953)

I made up this song like I was there on the spot, the day and the night it happened. This is the best way to make up a song like this.... Ludlow Massacre was one of the hundred battles fought to build trade unions. I want to sing a song to show our soldiers that Ludlow Massacres must not ever come back to us to kill 13 children and a pregnant woman, just to force you to work for cheap wages. (Woody Guthrie)

Colorado

By Woody Guthrie

I was worried bad about my children,
Soldiers guarding the railroad bridge;
Every once in a while the bullets would fly,
Kick up gravel under my feet.

We were so afraid you would kill our children,
We dug us a cave that was seven foot deep,
Carried our young ones and a pregnant woman
Down inside the cave to sleep.

That very night you soldiers waited,
Until us miners was asleep;
You snuck around our little tent town,
Soaked our tents with your kerosene.

You struck a match and the blaze it started;
You pulled the triggers of your gatling guns;
I made a run for the children but the fire wall stopped me,
Thirteen children died from your guns.

I carried my blanket to a wire fence corner,
Watched the fire till the blaze died down;
I helped some people grab their belongings,
While your bullets killed us all around.

I never will forget the look on the faces
Of the men and women that awful day,
When we stood around to preach their funerals,
And lay the corpses of the dead away.

We told the Colorado governor to phone the President,
Tell him to call off his National Guard;
But the National Guard belonged to the governor,
So he didn't try so very hard.

Our women from Trinidad they hauled some potatoes
Up to Walsenburg in a little cart;
They sold their potatoes and brought some guns back,
And they put a gun in every hand.

The state soldiers jumped us in the wire fence corner;
They did not know that we had these guns.
And the red-neck miners mowed down these troopers,
You should have seen those poor boys run.

We took some cement and walled the cave up,
Where you killed these thirteen children inside,
I said, "God bless the Mine Workers Union,"
And then I hung my head and cried.

Mine Workers and Their Families at the Beginning of Their Strike, Ludlow, Colorado. Courtesy of N.Y. Public Library Picture Collection.

I'm Off to Boise City

The Idaho gold rush of the 1860s attracted prospectors from all over, including old hands from the banks of the Sacramento. Boise itself thrived on whisky and gambling, with most financial transactions conducted in "dust." The saloons rang with music, including this takeoff of a blackface minstrel number of the 1850s, entitled "I'm Off for California." This would account for the implied Negro origins of the song in such lyrics as "The white folks must be crazy."

Idaho

Come gath – er 'round me, min – ers, I got some – thing for to ____ tell; Make you bust your brit – ches and cause your bos – om to swell. The white folks must be craz – y, the news it just ___ come out, The news from Boi – se Cit-y, _____ and it's com-in' from the south, ____

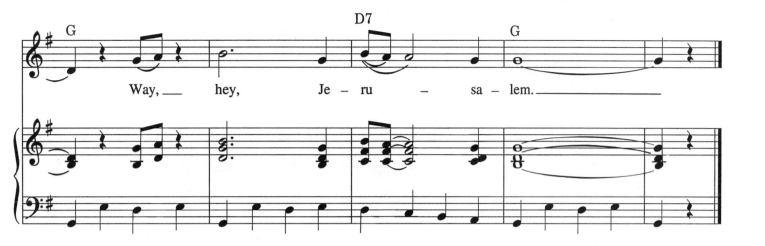

Way, ___ hey, Je – ru – sa-lem. ___

I have a wooden shovel, and another made of tin,
And the way I scoop that gravel up, it surely is a sin.
If them city white folks ask us who we be,
Just tell 'em it's the California Gold Mining Company.
Way, hey, Jerusalem.

I'm goin' downtown, the telegraph to hire,
And see if they need a colored man to greasen up the wire.
When I get down to Bannock, I'll take a cargo train,
Then on over to Centerville and I'll telegraph again.
Way, hey, Jerusalem.

Old Dan Tucker needn't want for his supper any more,
'Cause Abe's gonna take him down to that old Virginia shore.
I said, "So long and goodbye, my little Mary Blummer,
I'm off to Boise City, but I'll come back next summer."
Way, hey, Jerusalem.

The elephant ate his pot pie and danced with the crocodile,
Oh, Jerusalem, I am bound to go for a while.
I'm off to Boise City with a shovel and a hoe,
Pack up all your shiny clothes and we'll be on the go.
Way, hey, Jerusalem.

Silver City, Idaho. Courtesy of N.Y. Public Library Picture Collection.

Way Out in Idaho

The Oregon Short Line was completed in 1884. It ran from Pocatello through the Snake River Valley and up the Salmon River Mountains to Mackay. The building of this and other railways opened up the territory and facilitated increased quartz, lead, and silver mining.

Idaho

Come all you jol – ly rail – road men, and I'll sing you if I can, Of the

trials and trib – u – la – tions of a god – less rail – road man Who

start – ed out from Den-ver,_____ his for – ture to make grow, And

struck the Or – e – gon Short Line way out in I – da – ho. Way

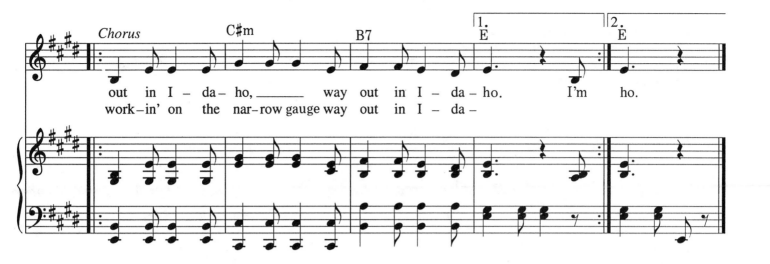

I was roaming around in Denver one luckless rainy day,
When Kilpatrick's man, Catcher, stepped up to me and did say,
"I'll lay you down five dollars as quickly as I can,
And you'll hurry up and catch the train, she's starting for Cheyenne." *Chorus*

He laid me down five dollars, like many another man,
And I started for the depot as happy as a clam;
When I got to Pocatello, my troubles began to grow,
A-wading through the sagebrush in frost and rain and snow. *Chorus*

When I got to American Falls, it was there I met Fat Jack.
He said he kept a hotel in a dirty canvas shack.
"We hear you are a stranger and perhaps your funds are low.
Well, yonder stands my hotel tent, the best in Idaho." *Chorus*

I followed my conductor into his hotel tent,
And for one square and hearty meal I paid him my last cent;
But Jack's a jolly fellow, and you'll always find him so,
A-workin' on the narrow-gauge way out in Idaho. *Chorus*

They put me to work next morning with a cranky cuss called Bill,
And they gave me a ten-pound hammer to strike upon a drill.
They said if I didn't like it I could take my shirt and go,
And they'd keep my blanket for my board way out in Idaho. *Chorus*

It filled my heart with pity as I walked along the track
To see so many old bummers with their turkeys on their backs.
They said the work was heavy and the grub they couldn't go.
Around Kilpatrick's tables way out in Idaho. *Chorus*

But now I'm well and happy, down in the harvest camps,
And there I will continue till I make a few more stamps.
I'll go down to New Mexico and I'll marry the girl I know,
And I'll buy me a horse and buggy and go back to Idaho. *Chorus*

I Ride an Old Paint

Cowboy lingo was a world unto itself: "paint" — a horse with irregular patterns of white and colored areas; "dan" — a dun-colored horse; "throw the houlihan" — bringing one's horse to an abrupt stop, thereby causing a roped animal to be thrown to the ground; "coulees" — dry creeks; "draw" — a shallow drain that catches rainfall; "fiery and snuffy" — spirited or wild cattle.

Montana

I ride an old paint, ___ I lead an old dan, ___ I'm goin' to Mon – tan – a to throw the hou – li – han. They feed in the cou – lees, they wa – ter in the draw; Their tails are all mat – ted, their backs are all raw.

Chorus

Ride a – round, lit – tle do – gies, Ride a – round ___ them __ slow, For the fier – y and snuf – fy are rar – in' to go.

Old Bill Jones had two daughters and a song,
One went to college the other went wrong,
His wife got killed in a pool-room fight,
But still he keeps singing from morning till night. *Chorus*

I've worked in the city, worked on the farm,
And all I've got to show is the muscle in my arm.
Patches on my pants, callous on my hand,
And I'm goin' to Montana to throw the houlihan. *Chorus*

When I die, don't bury me at all,
Put me on my pony and lead him from his stall.
Tie my bones to his back, turn our faces to the west,
And we'll ride the prairie that we love the best. *Chorus*

Custer's Last Charge

At the Little Bighorn River on June 25, 1876, General George A. Custer and a troop of 264 U.S. soldiers were annihilated by an overwhelming force of Sioux Indians under the leadership of chiefs Sitting Bull and Crazy Horse. It was a victory won by the Indians in a war doomed to be lost at the outset. Nothing the Indians could do could in reality stay the relentless tide of the white man as he moved ever westward, pushing, prodding, and killing them whenever they got in his way.

Montana

A – cross the Big Horn's crys-tal tide, a – gainst the sav–age Sioux. A

lit – tle band of sol – diers charged, three – hun – dred boys__ in blue. In

front rode blond–haired Cus-ter bold, pet of the wild __ fron – tier; A

he – ro of a hun–dred fights, his __ deeds known far and near.

"Charge, comrades, charge! There's death ahead, disgrace lurks in our rear!
Drive rowels deep! Come on, come on!" came his yells with ringing cheer.
And on the foe those heroes charged; there rose an awful yell,
It seemed as though those soldiers stormed the lowest gates of hell.

Three hundred rifles rattled forth, and torn was human form;
The black smoke rose in rolling waves above the leaden storm.
The death groans of the dying braves, their wounded piercing cries,
The hurling of the arrows fleet did cloud the noonday skies.

The snorting steeds with shrieks of fright, the firearms' deafening roar;
The war song sung by the dying braves who fell to rise no more.
O'er hill and dale the war song waved 'round craggy mountain side,
Along down death's dark valley ran a cruel crimson tide.

Our blond-haired chief was everywhere 'mid showers of hurling lead,
The starry banner waved above the dying and the dead.
With bridle rein in firm-set teeth, revolver in each hand,
He hoped with his few gallant boys to quell the great Sioux band.

Again they charged, three thousand guns poured forth their last-sent ball;
Three thousand war whoops rent the air; gallant Custer then did fall.
And all around where Custer fell ran pools and streams of gore,
Heaped bodies of both red and white whose last great fight was o'er.

The boys in blue and their savage foe lay huddled in one mass,
Their life's blood ran a-trickling through the trampled prairie grass,
While fiendish yells did rend the air and then a sudden hush,
While cries of anguish rise again as on the mad Sioux rush.

O'er those strewn and blood-stained fields those goading redskins fly;
Our gang went down three hundred souls, three hundred doomed to die,
Those blood-drunk braves sprang on the dead and wounded boys in blue,
Three hundred bleeding scalps ran high above the fiendish crew.

Then night came on with sable veil and hid those sights from view,
The Bighorn's crystal tide was red as she wound her valleys through.
And quickly from those fields of slain those gloating redskins fled,
But blond-haired Custer held the field, a hero with his dead.

All Are Talking of Utah

Utilizing the Civil War song "Marching Through Georgia" was a sure-fire way to get people to sing along. This song deals with the problems of polygamy and Utah's becoming a state.

Utah

Music by Henry C. Work
Words attributed to John Davis

Who'd ev – er think that U – tah would stir the world so much, Who'd ev – er think the Mor – mons were wide – ly known as such, I hard – ly dare to scrib – ble, or

'Tis Utah and the Mormons, in Congress, pulpit, press,
'Tis Utah and the Mormons, in every place, I guess;
We must be growing greater, we can't be growing less,
For all are talking of Utah. *Chorus*

They say they'll send an army to set the Mormons right,
Regenerate all Utah, and show us Christian light;
Release our wives and daughters, and put us men to fight,
For all are talking of Utah. *Chorus*

They say that Utah cannot be numbered as a State,
They wished our lands divided, but left it rather late;
'Tis hard to tell of Mormons, what yet may be their fate,
For all are talking of Utah. *Chorus*

Whatever may be coming, we cannot well foresee,
For it may be the Railroad, or some great prodigy;
At least the noted Mormons are watching what's to be,
For all are talking of Utah. *Chorus*

I now will tell you something you never thought of yet,
We bees are nearly filling the "Hive of Deseret."
If hurt we'll string together, and gather all we get,
For all are talking of Utah. *Chorus*

Saline, Utah, 1896. Courtesy of N.Y. Public Library Picture Collection.

The Bull Whacker

"Root Hog or Die" was a well-known song among the pioneers. It exists in many versions and parodies, but the message is always essentially the same — God helps them that help themselves — which translated into Pionerese as "Root, hog, or die." The Mormons moved the locale of one of these versions from the Denver Line to the Salt Lake Line.

Utah

It's not so very pleasant when you start upon the road,
With an awkward team and a very heavy load.
You have to whip and holler; if you swear it's on the sly.
Go it if you like it, boys, root, hog, or die.

Out upon the road you have to go it as you can,
They won't try to please you or any other man.
You have to go it night and day, also wet and dry,
Go it if you like it, boys, root, hog, or die.

Out upon the road it is a very hard task,
The worst thing of all we have so long to fast.
Only have two meals a day, the third passes you by.
You eat jerked meat and like it – root, hog, or die.

Perhaps you'd like to know, boys, what we have to eat,
A small piece of bread but a smaller piece of meat,
A little fruit and beans, sugar on the sly.
Go it if you like it, boys, root, hog, or die.

Perhaps you'd like to know, boys, what we have to sup,
We have a little coffee and an old rusty cup.
A little of the Platte, a little alkali,
Big pig, little pig, root, hog, or die.

All day long you must be upon your feet,
You'll see "root, hog, or die" marked on every wagon seat.
The dust within your throat, the sand within your eye,
You'll get enough of that, boys, root, hog, or die.

Every day at noon we have something to do.
And if it's nothing else, we have an ox to shoe.
With our ropes we throw him down, and there we make him lie
While we tack the shoes on, root, hog, or die.

There is a fine sight to be seen upon the road,
The antelope and deer and the big sandy toad.
The elk and buffalo, the rabbits jump so high,
And the bloody redskins – root, hog, or die.

We arrived in Salt Lake City on the twenty-fourth of July,
The folks were all surprised for to see us coming by.
We are jovial bull whackers on whom you can rely.
We're tough and can stand it, boys, root, hog, or die.

Oldest House in Salt Lake City, Built in 1847. Courtesy of N.Y. Public Library Picture Collection.

The Wyoming Nester

The plea for friendship between the cowboy and the farmer in the Broadway musical *Oklahoma!* was an echo of the real conflict that had developed by the 1880s as the human tide of hungry land seekers began fencing in open cattle range. For over a decade the battles raged — for battles they indeed were at times — until, as it had to be, the settlers won. The days of the open range were gone forever.

Wyoming

"Here's luck to all you home - stead - ers, _____ You've tak - en this coun - try at last, _____ And I hope you suc - ceed in the fu - ture, _____ As the cow - boys done in the past. _____

"You've homesteaded all of this country,
Where the slicks and the mavericks did roam;
You've driven me far from my country,
Far from my birthplace and home.

"The cattle are still getting thinner,
And the ranches are shorter on men,
But I've got me a full quart of whisky
And nearly a full quart of gin.

"You have taken up all of the water,
And all of the land that's nearby"—
And he took a big drink from his bottle
Of good old '99 rye.

He rode far into the evening,
His limbs at last had grown tired.
He shifted himself in his saddle,
And he slowly hung down his head.

His saddle he used for a pillow;
His blanket he used for a bed.
As he lay himself down for a night's slumber,
These words to himself he then said:

"I'm leaving Wyoming forever,
This land and the home of my birth,
It fills my heart with sorrow,
But it fills your heart with mirth."

Statehood Parade, 1890.

Wyoming Statehood Parade, 1890. Courtesy of N.Y. Public Library Picture Collection.

206

Good-Bye, Old Paint

The cowboy — the sentimental cowboy — sang this farewell song at the end of a rare evening in town, at a cowboy dance. It was the last waltz.

Wyoming

D.C. al Fine

Old Paint's a good pony, he paces when he can,
Good-bye, little Annie, I'm off for Cheyenne.   *Chorus*

Oh, hitch up your horses and feed 'em some hay,
And seat yourself by me so long as you stay.   *Chorus*

My horses ain't hungry, they'll not eat your hay,
My wagon is loaded and rolling away.   *Chorus*

My foot in the stirrup, the reins in my hands,
Good morning, young lady, my horses won't stand.   *Chorus*

Cheyenne Express Line, Wyoming, 1884. Courtesy of N.Y. Public Library Picture Collection.

Pacific

Pacific

Grand Coulee Dam. Courtesy of N.Y. Public Library Picture Collection.

The Klondike Gold Rush

Gold, that great people-mover of the 19th century, was discovered on Forty Mile Creek in 1887 and over the border on the Canadian side at Klondike in 1896. The gold rush to the frozen North, with the enormous difficulties of weather and terrain, rivaled anything that had previously been experienced in the "Lower 48." The geographical term "Klondike" was loosely applied to both the Alaskan and Yukon diggings. The Alaska Historical Library, in its brochure *Musical Reflections of Alaska's History*, lists a number of "Klondike" songs, including "The Belle of Klondike" (1898), "Klondike or Bust" (1897), and "To Klondike We've Paid Our Fare" (1897).

Alaska

210

The Cremation Of Sam McGee

A bunch of the boys were whooping it up in the Malamute saloon;
The kid that handles the music box was hitting a jag-time tune;
Back of the bar, in a solo game, sat Dangerous Dan McGrew;
And watching his luck was his light-o'-love, the lady that's known as Lou.

So begins Robert W. Service's other great epic fantasy of Alaskan prospectors, gamblers, and their ladies, "The Shooting of Dan McGrew." Service's imagination and gift for language peopled his poems of the gold-rush days with wonderfully realistic, yet improbable characters and situations.

Alaska

Words by Robert W. Service
Music by Jerry Silverman

There are strange things done in the mid-night sun by the men who moil for gold; The__

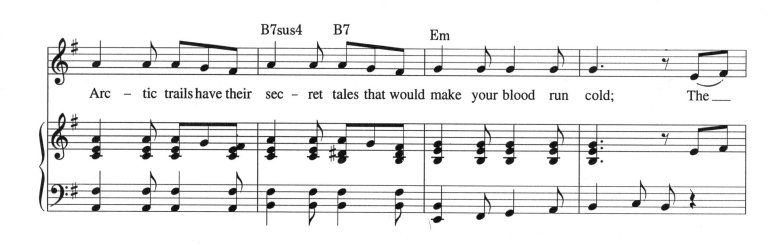

Arc-tic trails have their sec-ret tales that would make your blood run cold; The__

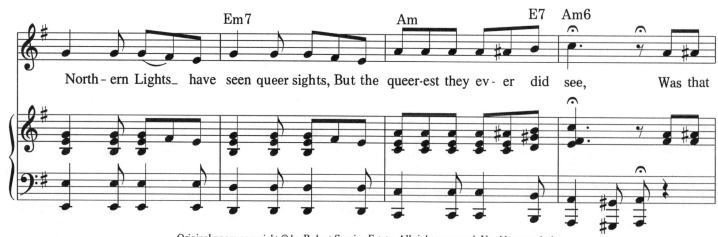

North-ern Lights_ have seen queer sights, But the queer-est they ev-er did see, Was that

All the verses are sung to this melody

night on the marge ___ of Lake ___ Le-barge ___ I cre-mat-ed Sam Mc-Gee. _____ Now __

Sam Mc-Gee was from Ten – nes-see, where the cot - ton blooms and blows, Why he

left his home in the South to roam 'round the Pole, God on – ly knows. He was

al – ways cold, but the land of gold seemed to hold him like a spell; Though he'd

of – ten say in his home – ly way that he'd "soon – er live in hell."

On a Christmas Day we were mushing our way over the Dawson trail.
Talk of your cold! through the parka's fold it stabbed like a driven nail.
If our eyes we'd close, then the lashes froze till sometimes we couldn't see;
It wasn't much fun, but the only one to whimper was Sam McGee.

And that very night, as we lay packed tight in our robes beneath the snow,
And the dogs were fed, and the stars o'erhead were dancing heel and toe,
He turned to me, and "Cap," says he, "I'll cash in this trip, I guess;
And if I do, I'm asking that you won't refuse my last request."

Well, he seemed so low that I couldn't say no; then he says with a sort of moan:
"It's the cursed cold, and it's got right hold till I'm chilled clean through to the bone.
Yet 'tain't being dead – it's my awful dread of the icy grave that pains;
So I want you to swear that, foul or fair, you'll cremate my last remains."

A pal's last need is a thing to heed, so I swore I would not fail;
And we started on at the streak of dawn; but God! he looked ghastly pale.
He crouched on the sleigh, and he raved all day of his home in Tennessee;
And before nightfall a corpse was all that was left of Sam McGee.

With a corpse half hid that I couldn't get rid, I hurried, horror-driven,
There wasn't a breath in that land of death, and because of a promise given,
It was lashed to the sleigh, and it seemed to say: "You may tax your brawn and brains,
But you promised true, and it's up to you to cremate those last remains."

Now a promise made is a debt unpaid, and the trail has its own stern code.
In the days to come, though my lips were dumb, in my heart how I cursed that load.
In the long, long night, by the lone firelight, while the huskies, round in a ring,
Howled out their woes to the homeless snows, O God! how I loathed the thing.

And every day that quiet clay seemed to heavy and heavier grow;
And on I went, though the dogs were spent and the grub was getting low;
The trail was bad, and I felt half mad, but I swore I would not give in;
And I'd often sing to the hateful thing, and it hearkened with a grin.

Till I came to the marge of Lake Lebarge, and a derelict there lay;
It was jammed in the ice, but I saw in a trice it was called the *Alice May*.
And I looked at it, and I thought a bit, and I looked at my frozen chum;
Then "Here," said I, with a sudden cry, "is my cre-ma-tor-eum."

Some planks I tore from the cabin floor, and I lit the boiler fire;
Some coal I found that was lying around, and I heaped the fuel higher;
The flames just roared, and the furnace roared such a blaze you seldom see;
And I burrowed a hole in the glowing coal, and I stuffed in Sam McGee.

Then I made a hike, for I didn't like to hear him sizzle so;
And the heavens scowled, and the huskies howled, and the wind began to blow.
It was icy cold, but the hot sweat rolled down my cheeks, and I don't know why;
And the greasy smoke in an inky cloak went streaking down the sky.

I do not know how long in the snow I wrestled with grisly fear;
But the stars came out and they danced about 'ere again I ventured near;
I was sick with dread, but I bravely said: "I'll just take a peep inside.
I guess he's cooked, and it's time I looked"; then the door I opened wide.

And there sat Sam, looking cool and calm, in the heart of the furnace roar;
And he wore a smile you could see a mile, and he said: "Please close that door.
It's fine in here, but I greatly fear you'll let in the cold and storm.
Since I left Plumtree, down in Tennessee, it's the first time I've been warm."

Alaska. 1898. Courtesy of N.Y. Public Library Picture Collection.

Life In California

The first of the many gold-rush minstrels was Dr. D. G. ("Doc") Robinson, who arrived in San Francisco from his native Maine on January 1, 1849. His satirical songs lampooned bigwigs, phonies, and self-important dandies who couldn't pay their bills. This, his most popular number, borrowed the melody from William Henry Harrison's campaign song "Van, Van, He's a Used-Up Man," which helped defeat Martin Van Buren in the presidential election of 1840.

California

By D. G. Robinson

Oh, I ain't got no home, nor ___ noth-ing else I s'pose, Mis-
come to Cal - i - forn' with a heart both stout and bold, I've

for - tune seems to fol - low me where - ev - er I goes. I
been up to the dig - gings there to get me some gold. But

Chorus

I'm a used – up man, a per - fect used - up man, And if

ev - er I get home a – gain, I'll stay there if I can.

I lives way down in Maine, where I heard about the diggings,
So I shipped aboard a darned old barque, commanded by Joe Higgins;
I sold my little farm and from wife and children parted,
And off to California sailed, and left 'em broken hearted.   *Chorus*

When I got to San Francisco, I saw such heaps of money,
And the way the folks monte played, I thought the game quite funny;
So I took my little pile, and on the table tossed it,
And the chap who dealt me out the cards says, "My friend, you have lost it!"   *Chorus*

I got into a steamboat and started up the river,
When I thought the darned mosquitoes would ha' taken out my liver;
When I got to Sacramento, I buckled on this rigging,
And soon I found a decent place, and so I went to digging.   *Chorus*

I got into the water where the "fever-n-ager" took me,
And after I was froze to death, it turned about and shook me;
But still I kept to work, a-hopin' 'twould be better,
But the water wouldn't fall a bit, but kept a-getting wetter.   *Chorus*

I 'spose if I should die, they'd take me to the Mission,
Or else Jim Riddle'd sell me off to pay up my physician;
I've tried to keep up courage, and swore I wouldn't spree it,
And here's my pile for five months' work, I'd lief as not you'd see it.   *Chorus*

I don't know what to do, for all the time I'm dodging
To hunt up grub enough to eat, and find a decent lodging;
I can't get any liquor and no one seems to meet me
Who'll take me by the collar now, and kindly ask to treat me!   *Chorus*

I'll go up to the "Woodcock," and see if Tom won't trust me,
For Tom has got too good a heart, I'm sure, to try to bust me;
But if they shouldn't know me there, or say I can't be trusted,
Why then, kind friends, without your help, the poor old miner's busted.   *Chorus*

I don't know how it is, but I've a dreadful feeling,
If I don't get some business soon, I'll have to take to stealing;
I'd like some city office here, and the tax law wants correcting,
I'd make a first-rate Mayor, too, and only want electing.   *Chorus*

But to my friends I see tonight, my thanks, I can't express 'em,
And for their generosity, can only say, God bless 'em!
For what of kindness they don't know, I'm sure ain't worth the knowing,
So with my warmest thanks, kind friends, I think I'll be a-going.   *Chorus*

Do Re Mi

Our next guest really has traveled. He is Woody Guthrie of Oklahoma, one of those Okies who, dispossessed from their farms, journeyed in jalopies to California. There, Woody, who always had been a great man at playing the guitar and making up songs of his own, managed to get some work performing at a small radio station. He got a lot of fan letters, one was from John Steinbeck, who wrote the saga of the Okies. Not long ago, he set out for New York and rode the freights to get here...and we've asked him to perform one of his own compositions. We present Woody Guthrie and "If You Ain't Got the Do Re Mi." (Burgess Meredith introducing Woody on the CBS radio program *The Pursuit of Happiness*, April 20, 1941; quoted in *Woody Guthrie, A Life* by Joe Klein, 1980)

California

By Woody Guthrie

Lots of folks back east they say, Leav-ing home ev-'ry day,

Beat-ing a hot old dust-y way to the Cal – i-for – nia line.

'Cross the des – ert sands they roll, Get-ting out of that old dust bowl,

boys, If you ain't got the do re mi, _____ Why, you bet-ter get back to beau-ti – ful Tex – as, _____ Ok – la – ho – ma, Kan – sas, Geor-gia, Ten – nes- see. _____ Cal – i – for – nia's a Gar – den of

If you want to buy a house or farm,
That can't do nobody harm,
Or take your vacation by the mountain or sea.
Don't swap your old cow for a car,
You'd better stay right where you are;
Better take this little tip from me.
'Cause I look through the want ads every day,
But the headlines in the papers always say, *Chorus*

Rolling Down to Old Maui

In her book *Songs of American Sailormen* (1938), Joanna Colcord writes: "I have been unable to find anyone who recalls the air to which this fine old song was sung. It was a favorite with the "bow-head" whalemen, who were accustomed to put in at the Hawaiian Islands on the homeward voyage, after a season spent in hunting their prey amid the ice-floes of the Arctic." In an attempt to recreate this "fine old song," I have set the words to an original melody based on the style of songs of the period.

Hawaii

Music by Jerry Silverman

i. Roll-ing down to old Mau - i, my boys, Roll-ing down to old Mau - i. But

now we're bound to the Arc - tic ground, Roll-ing down to old Mau - i.

We will heave our lead where old Diamond Head
  Looms up on old Oahu,
Our masts and rigging are covered with ice,
  Our decks are filled with snow.
The hoary head of the Sea Gull Isles,
  That decks the Arctic Sea,
Are many and many leagues astern,
  Since we steered for old Maui.   *Chorus*

O welcome the seas and the fragrant breeze,
  Laden with odors rare,
And the pretty maids in the sunny glades,
  Who are gentle, kind and fair,
And their pretty eyes even now look out,
  Hoping some day to see
Our snow-white sails before the gales,
  Rolling down to old Maui.   *Chorus*

Once more we sail with a favoring gale,
  Toward our distant home.
Our mainmast sprung, we're almost done,
  Still we ride the ocean's foam.
Our stun' sail booms are carried away,
  What care we for that sound,
A living gale is after us,
  Hurrah, we're homeward bound.   *Chorus*

Little Mohee

Those same Arctic whalers who sang the preceding song also sang this one. The woman in question, Little Mohee (sometimes spelled "Mohea"), was a native of Maui — which was pronounced "Mohee" by the sailors.

Hawaii

224

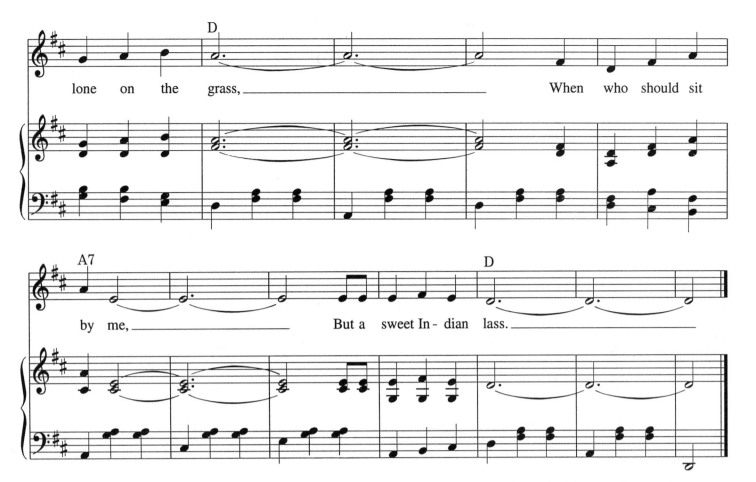

lone　on　the　grass,＿＿＿＿＿＿＿＿＿＿＿＿＿＿ When　who　should　sit

by　me,＿＿＿＿＿＿＿＿＿＿ But a　sweet In - dian　lass.＿＿＿＿＿＿＿＿＿＿

She sat down beside me upon a fine day,
I got awful lonesome as the day passed away,
She asked me to marry, and gave me her hand,
Said, "My pappy's a chieftain all over this land."

"My pappy's a chieftain and ruler be he,
I'm his only daughter and my name is Mohee."
I answered and told her that it never could be,
'Cause I had my own sweetheart in my own country.

I had my own sweetheart and I knew she loved me.
Her heart was as true as any Mohee.
So I said, "I must leave you and goodbye my dear,
There's a wind in my canvas and home I must steer."

At home with relations I tried for to see,
But there wasn't one there like my little Mohee;
And the girl I had trusted proved untrue to me,
So I sailed o'er the ocean to my little Mohee.

Acres of Clams

The Irish song "Old Rosin, the Beau" contributed its melody to this American pioneer's tale of hard times, which uncharacteristically winds up with a happy ending.

Washington

Bm　A7　D

sold.　　　　I've　tun – nelled, hy ___ drau – licked and　cra – dled,

G　D　A7　D

And　　I　have　been　fre – quent – ly　sold. _____

For one who gets riches by mining,
Perceiving that hundreds grow poor,
I made up my mind to try farming,
The only pursuit that is sure.

Chorus: The only pursuit that is sure, (2)
　　　　　I made up my mind to try farming,
　　　　　The only pursuit that is sure.

So, rolling my grub in a blanket,
I left my tools on the ground.
And I started one morning to shank it
For the country they call Puget Sound.

Chorus: For the country...

Arriving flat broke in midwinter,
The ground was enveloped in fog;
And covered all over with timber
Thick as hair on the back of a dog.

Chorus: Thick as hair...

When I looked at the prospects so gloomy
The tears trickled over my face;
And I thought that my travels had brought me
To the end of the jumping-off place.

Chorus: To the end...

I staked me a claim in the forest
And set myself down to hard toil.
For two years I chopped and I struggled,
But I never got down to the soil.

Chorus: But I never...

I tried to get out of the country,
But poverty forced me to stay.
Until I became an old settler,
Then nothing could drive me away.

Chorus: Then nothing...

And now that I'm used to the country,
I think that if man ever found
A place to live easy and happy,
That Eden is on Puget Sound.

Chorus: That Eden...

No longer the slave of ambition.
I laugh at the world and is shams;
As I think of my happy condition,
Surrounded by acres of clams.

Chorus: Surrounded by acres...

227

The Biggest Thing That Man Has Ever Done

In casting about for superlatives to describe the Grand Coulee Dam, Woody borrowed the idea of the historical traveler who has been everywhere and seen and done everything worth doing from the song "I Was Born About Ten Thousand Years Ago." His genius has placed this song (and all his other songs) among the ranks of true American folk songs.

Washington

By Woody Guthrie

I worked in the Garden of Eden, 'twas in the year of two,
Join'd the apple pickers union, I always paid my due;
I'm the man that signed the contract to raise the rising sun,
And that was about the biggest thing that man had ever done.

I was straw boss on the pyramids, the Tower of Babel, too,
I opened up the ocean, let the migrant children through;
I fought a million battles and I never lost a one,
Well, that was about the biggest thing that man had ever done.

I beat the daring Roman, I beat the daring Turk,
I defeated Nero's army with thirty minutes work;
I stopped the mighty Kaiser, and stopped the mighty Hun,
And that was about the biggest thing that man had ever done.

I was in the revolution when we set the country free,
Me and a couple of Indians that dumped the Boston tea;
We won the battle at Valley Forge, and battle of Bull Run,
And that was about the biggest thing that man had ever done.

Next we won the slavery war, some other fella and me,
And every slave in Dixie was freed by U. S. G.
The slavery men had lost the war, the freedom men had won,
And that was about the biggest thing that man had ever done.

And then I took to farming on the great midwestern plain,
The dust it blowed a hundred years, but never come a rain
Well, me and a million other fellas left there on the run,
And that was about the biggest thing that man has ever done.

I clumb the rocky canyon where the Columbia River rolls,
Seen the salmon leaping the rapids and the falls;
The big Grand Coulee Dam in the state of Washington
Is just about the biggest thing that man has ever done.

There's a building in New York that you call the Empire State,
I rode the rods to 'Frisco to walk the Golden Gate;
I've seen every foot of film that Hollywood has run,
But Coulee is the biggest thing that man has ever done.

Three times the size of Boulder or the highest pyramid,
Makes the Tower of Babel a plaything for a kid;
From the rising of the river to the setting of the sun,
The Coulee is the biggest thing that man has ever done.

I better quit my talking 'cause I told you all I know,
But please remember, pardner, wherever you may go,
I been from here to yonder, I been from sun to sun,
But Coulee Dam's the biggest thing that man has ever done.

There's a man across the ocean, boys, I guess you now him well,
His name is Adolf Hitler, we'll blow his soul to hell;
We'll kick him in the panzers and put him on the run,
And that'll be the biggest thing that man has ever done.

Roll On, Columbia

This song was wrote up by an Okie passing through your country, and I'm pretty certain that everybody just first a-coming into this country has got some such similar song in his or her head, but times is such that they just can't sing it out loud, so you might not hear it. (Woody Guthrie, outskirts of Portland, Oregon; May 12, 1941)

Oregon

By Woody Guthrie
3rd verse by Michael Loring

lum – bia, roll on; Your pow – er is turn – ing the dark – ness to

dawn – It's roll on, Co–lum – bia, roll on.

Other great rivers add power to you,
Yakima, Snake, and the Klickitat, too,
Sandy, Willamette, and Hood River, too;
Roll on Columbia, roll on!   *Chorus*

Tom Jefferson's vision would not let him rest,
An empire he saw in the Pacific Northwest.
Sent Lewis and Clark and they did the rest;
Roll on, Columbia, Roll On!   *Chorus*

It's there on your banks that we fought many a fight,
Sheridan's boys in the block house that night,
They saw us in death, but never in flight;
Roll on, Columbia, Roll On!   *Chorus*

At Bonneville now there are ships in the locks,
The waters have risen and cleared all the rocks,
Ship loads of plenty will steam past the docks,
So, Roll on, Columbia, Roll On!   *Chorus*

And on up the river at Grand Coulec dam,
The mightiest thing ever built by a man,
To run to great factories for old Uncle Sam;
It's roll on, Columbia, roll on!   *Chorus*

That Oregon Trail

In the mountains of north California (May 1941) we got a registered letter that told us to come up to the Columbia River to the Bonneville and the Grand Coulee dam, to the office of the Bonneville Power Administration. Well, I talked to people, I got my job, it was to read some books about the Coulee and Bonneville dams, to walk around up and down the rivers, and to see what I could find to make up songs about. I made up 26. They played them over the loudspeakers at meetings to sell bonds to carry the high lines from the dams to the little towns. The private power dams hated to see these two babies born to stand up out there across those rockwall canyons, and they pulled every trick possible to hold up the deal, saying that the materials would be wasted and could be used to build a big war machine to beat Hitler with. Our argument was that we could run a thousand towns and factories, farms, with these two power dams, and turn out aluminum bombers to beat Hitler a lot quicker with. And our side won out on top.
(Woody Guthrie)

Oregon

By Woody Guthrie

I been a – grub-bin' on a lit-tle farm___ on the flat and win-dy plains,___ I been a – list-'nin' to the hun-gry cat-tle bawl.

pack my wife and kids,___ I'm gon-na hit that west-ern road,___ I'm gon-na

I'm gon-na hit that O-re-gun Trail_ this com-in' fall.

Well my land is dry and cracklin'
And my chickens they're a cacklin'
'Cause this dirt and dust is gettin' in their craw.
They been laying' flint rock eggs,
I got to bust 'em with a sledge;
I got to hit that Oregon trail this comin' fall.   *Chorus*

Yes, my hogs and pigs are squealin',
They're a rockin' and a reelin',
'Cause there ain't no mud to waller in the draw.
I'm a gonna grab them by their tails,
Take them down that western trail,
I'm gonna hit that Oregon trail this comin' fall. *Chorus*

Well, my good old horse is bony,
And he's tired and lonesome too;
You can count his ribs three quarters of a mile.
Throw my bedroll on his back,
Both the bay horse and the black;
I'm gonna hit that Oregon trail this comin' fall.   *Chorus*

Now, my true love she gets ailin',
When this dry old dust gets sailin',
And she wishes for the days beyond recall.
If we work hard there's a future
In that north Pacific land;
I'm gonna hit that Oregon trail this comin' fall.   *Chorus*

Courtesy of N.Y. Public Library Picture Collection.

234

Index

Bostonians Observing the Battle of Bunker Hill, June 16, 1775. Courtesy of N.Y. Public Library Picture Collection.

Everybody's Music Teacher